Module 9

Teaching Beginning Spellin

LETRS

Language Essentials
for Teachers of
Reading and
Spelling

Louisa C. Moats, Ed.D.

SOPRIS WEST™ EDUCATIONAL SERVICES
A CAMBIUM LEARNING COMPANY

BOSTON, MA • LONGMONT, CO

ISBN 1-59318-197-3

Printed in the United States of America

Published and Distributed by

SOPRIS
WEST™
EDUCATIONAL SERVICES

A Cambium Learning™ Company

4093 Specialty Place • Longmont, CO 80504 • (303) 651-2829
www.sopriswest.com

191MOD9/11-05

Dedication

To my husband, Steve Mitchell, whose support is constant and invaluable.

Acknowledgments

The LETRS modules have been developed with the help of many people. Our active national trainers, including Carol Tolman, Susan Hall, Marsha Davidson, Anne Cunningham, Marcia Berger, Deb Glaser, Linda Farrell, Judi Dodson, and Anne Whitney have all offered valuable suggestions for improving the module content and structure. Their devotion to delivering LETRS across the country is appreciated beyond measure. Bruce Rosow, Kevin Feldman, Susan Lowell, Patricia Mathes, Marianne Steverson, Lynn Kuhn, Jan Hasbrouck, and Nancy Eberhardt contributed their expertise to the first edition and continue to provide essential input and feedback. Many other professionals from all over the country who have attended institutes and offered constructive criticism have enabled our response to educators. I hope you see your ideas reflected in the revised editions of this continually evolving material.

I am grateful for the daily support and energy of the Sopris West office staff, editors, and designers including Lynne Stair, Sue Campbell, Sandra Knauke, Christine Kosmicki, and Kim Harris. Special thanks are due to Toni Backstrom, who manages the LETRS program with enthusiasm, competence, and commitment.

Stu Horsfall, Ray Beck, Steve Mitchell, Chet Foraker, and Steve Kukic are the vision and energy behind the publication of evidence-based programs in education that will help all children learn. I am so fortunate to be working with all of you.

—LCM

About the Author

Louisa C. Moats, Ed.D., is a nationally recognized authority on how children learn to read and why people fail to learn to read. Widely acclaimed as a researcher, speaker, consultant, and trainer, Dr. Moats has developed the landmark professional development program LETRS for teachers and reading specialists. She recently completed four years as site director of the NICHD Early Interventions Project in Washington, D.C., which included daily work with inner city teachers and children. This longitudinal, large-scale project was conducted through the University of Texas, Houston; it investigated the causes and remedies for reading failure in high-poverty urban schools. Dr. Moats spent the previous fifteen years in private practice as a licensed psychologist in Vermont, specializing in evaluation and consultation with individuals of all ages who experienced difficulty with reading, spelling, writing, and oral language.

Dr. Moats began her professional career as a neuropsychology technician and teacher of students with learning disabilities. She later earned her master's degree at Peabody College of Vanderbilt University and her doctorate in reading and human development from the Harvard Graduate School of Education. She has been licensed to teach in three states. Louisa has been an adjunct professor of psychiatry at Dartmouth Medical School and clinical associate professor of pediatrics at the University of Texas at Houston.

In addition to LETRS (Sopris West, 2004), her authored and co-authored books include:

- *Speech to Print: Language Essentials for Teachers* (Brookes Publishing, 2000),

- *Spelling: Development, Disability, and Instruction* (York Press, 1995),

- *Straight Talk About Reading* (Contemporary Books, 1998),

- *Parenting A Struggling Reader* (Random House, 2002),

- *Spellography* (Sopris West, 2003),

- *TRIP: The Reading Intervention Program* (Sopris West, in development).

Louisa has also published numerous journal articles, chapters, and policy papers including the American Federation of Teachers' "Teaching Reading is Rocket Science," the Learning First Alliance's "Every Child Reading: A Professional Development Guide," and the report on the D.C. Early Interventions Project: "Conditions for Sustaining Research-Based Practices in Early Reading Instruction" (with Barbara Foorman), *Journal of Remedial and Special Education*, 2004. She continues to dedicate her professional work to the improvement of teacher preparation and professional development. She is the consulting director of literacy research and professional development for Sopris West Educational Services. Louisa and her husband divide their time between homes in Colorado, Idaho, and Vermont. Their extended family includes a professional skier, a school psychologist, an alpaca rancher, and an Australian Shepherd.

Contents for Module 9

Overview of LETRS: Language Essentials for Teachers of Reading and Spelling

LETRS is designed to enrich and extend, but not to replace, program-specific professional development for teachers of reading and language arts. Teachers who implement a core, comprehensive reading program must know the format and instructional routines necessary to implement daily lessons. Teaching reading is complex and demanding, and new teachers will need both modeling and classroom coaching to implement the program well. Program-specific training, however, is not enough to enable teachers to tailor instruction to the diverse needs in their classrooms. Even teachers who are getting good results will need to understand the research-based principles of reading development, reading differences, and reading instruction. Reaching *all* learners through assessment and intervention is only possible when the teacher understands who is having difficulty, why they might be struggling, and what approaches to intervention are grounded in evidence. An empowered teacher is one who knows and can implement the best practices of the field, as established by a scientific research consensus.

The American Federation of Teachers' *Teaching Reading Is Rocket Science* and the Learning First Alliance's *Every Child Reading: A Professional Development Guide* provided the blueprint for these modules. LETRS modules teach concepts about language structure, reading development, reading difficulty, and assessment practices that guide research-based instruction. The format of instruction in LETRS allows for deep learning and reflection beyond the brief "once over" treatment the topics are typically given. Our professional development approach has been successful with diverse groups of teachers: regular classroom and special education, novice and expert, rural and urban.

The modules address each component of reading instruction in depth—phonological and phonemic awareness; phonics, decoding, spelling, and word study; oral language development; vocabulary; reading fluency; comprehension; and writing—as well as the links among these components. The characteristics and the needs of second language learners (ELL), dialect speakers, and students with other learning differences are woven into the modules. Assessment modules teach a problem-solving strategy for grouping children and designing instruction.

Teachers usually need extended time to learn and apply the knowledge and skills included in LETRS, depending on their background and experience. The content is dense by design. Each module is written so that teacher participants will engage in questions, problems, and tasks that lead to understanding, but understanding may occur in small steps, gradually, over several years. Some of the modules also are accompanied by

the LETRS Interactive CD-ROMS, self-instructional supplements for independent study and practice, developed with the help of a grant from the SBIR program of the National Institute for Child Health and Human Development.

More information about LETRS material, programs, and institutes is available at www.letrs.com.

Content of LETRS Modules Within the Language-Literacy Connection

Components of Comprehensive Reading Instruction	Organization of Language						
	Phonology	Morphology	Orthography	Semantics	Syntax	Discourse and Pragmatics	Etymology
Phonological Awareness	2	2					
Phonics, Spelling, and Word Study	3, 7	3, 7, 10	3, 7, 10				3, 10
Fluency	5		5	5	5		
Vocabulary	4	4	4	4	4		4
Text Comprehension		6		6	6	6, 11	
Written Expression			9, 11	9, 11	9, 11	9, 11	
Assessment	8, 12	8, 12	8, 12	8, 12	8, 12	8, 12	

Objectives

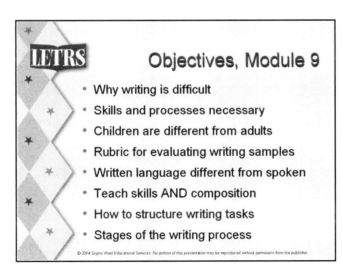

Slide 1

◆ Understand and summarize the cognitive processes employed during writing

◆ Discuss and describe examples of young children's writing

◆ Consider the difference between children's writing processes and those of adults

◆ Review the special qualities of written language

◆ Appreciate the importance of handwriting, spelling, and sentence fluency for composition quality and length

◆ Explore the progression of children's writing development in grades K-2

◆ Review a lesson format that balances skills with composition

◆ Learn how to structure the stages of the writing process for young writers

◆ Role-play various writing tasks appropriate for first and second grade

© The New Yorker Collection 1986 by Richard Cline. Reprinted with permission.

"Sorry, but I'm ging to have to issue you a summons for reckless grammar and driving without an apostrophe."

Writing Is Important

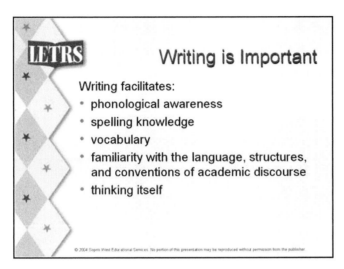

Slide 2

Although written expression was not one of the "critical components" of reading listed in the Reading First or Reading Excellence initiatives, and the National Reading Panel Report (2000) does not include a section on writing, writing is an essential component of a comprehensive literacy program. Reading comprehension is enhanced when students write a response to their reading.[1] Phonological awareness and attention to the details of print occur when children spell. Word choice during writing promotes vocabulary development. Mastery of sentence structure, metaphoric language, text organization, and voice is the product of writing even more than of reading. Writers are more intimate with language forms they have used themselves than they are with language they have merely encountered during reading.

When students write about their experiences and ideas, they engage both personal and objective meanings at the deepest level. As writers, we talk with ourselves and to others about what we believe, and in so doing, discover much about what we know to be true. Learning to write, however, is a protracted and challenging process.

---

[1] See S. Stotsky (2001), *Writing: The Road to Reading Comprehension.*

Writing Is Difficult

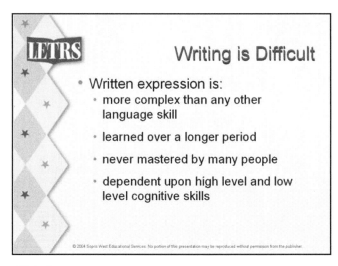

Slide 3

The production of written language is the latest developing, most challenging form of language use in humans. Adults who can read are often much less skilled at writing clearly. Many children who read well have difficulty learning to write. The act of composing and transcribing written language draws on all the processing systems needed for reading and on many others as well. A writer uses not only the four processors critical for word recognition (phonological, orthographic, meaning, and context) but also draws heavily on other language, motor, memory, attention, and executive functions.[2] Writing is like juggling many balls at once—most in the mind, a few in the hand.

Preparation for writing begins long before children reach kindergarten. Development of writing skill continues for many years. What educators do to nurture writing growth in young primary children must be guided by our most current and credible research on children's writing development.[3]

---

[2] Executive functions are those cognitive functions in charge of inhibition, initiation, shifting from one thing to another, and sustaining attention until a goal is achieved.

[3] The research on which this module is based has been conducted by interdisciplinary teams of researchers associated primarily with the University of Washington, Seattle, where brain imaging, performance measurement, instructional interventions and sophisticated statistical modeling of component processes in learning have been systematically linked (see Berninger & Richards, 2002).

LETRS

Writing is A Juggling Act

High Level Thinking	Lower Level Skills
• Logical connections among ideas	• Letter formation
• Control over genre structure	• Sound-spelling links
• Maintenance of a writing goal	• Recall of sight words
• Keeping the reader's needs in mind	• Use of punctuation and capitalization
	• Monitoring of symbolic accuracy

© 2004 Sopris West Educational Services. No portion of this presentation may be reproduced without permission from the publisher.

Slide 4

What Good Writers Know and Do

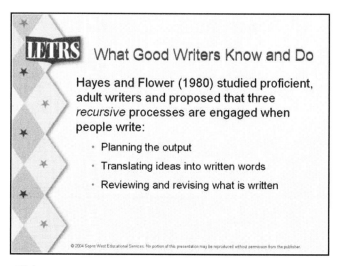

Slide 5

In 1980, Hayes and Flower explained the mental activities of adult writers in a way that heavily influenced writing education at the time. Hayes and Flower offered a conceptual model of writing that was derived from the self-reports of college students who verbalized their own thinking processes as they composed. On the basis of these data, Hayes and Flowers maintained that there were three major sub-domains of written expression that worked recursively with one another during writing. All processes could be active at any time:

Planning the writing;
Translating words into text;
Reviewing and changing drafts.

Hayes and Flower's portrait of the mental juggling act of writing heavily influenced educational practice. It contributed to the view that writing instruction should emphasize processes such as brainstorming and generating ideas, producing a series of drafts, interacting with an audience in order to revise and improve the composition, and using publication as the motivator to edit for writing conventions.

Slide 6

Young Children Are Different From Adults

After 20 years of additional studies of young children's writing development, however, researchers have shown that young children's writing processes are significantly different from those of competent adults. The translating component of writing accounts for much of the variability in the competence of young children but it received little special emphasis in Hayes and Flower's studies of adults. Whereas skilled writers already have learned how to translate ideas into words and write them down, beginning writers must acquire many specific skills before they can manage higher level composing tasks and lower level transcription tasks simultaneously.

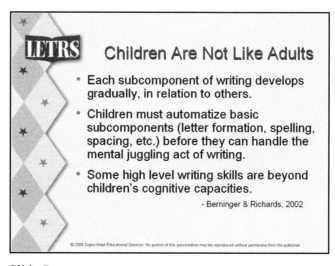

Slide 7

Multiple components of the writing process develop gradually and sequentially in the early grades. The three major components proposed by Hayes and Flower all can be addressed in early writing instruction, but with planned orchestration that will emphasize critical skills in critical periods of development, and that will enable eventual integration of these skills in academic writing. The three phases of the writing process are elaborated below in light of their relative importance in a beginning writing program.[4] Before we consider what young children need, however, consider what children's writing itself can tell us about their instructional needs.

Exercise #1: Describing Children's Writing Samples

Look over and describe these writing samples through whatever "lens" you already use. Do you work with a rubric that helps you judge the writing according to patterns in children's writing development? Do you see evidence that any of the children face special challenges in writing, even though you know nothing else about them?

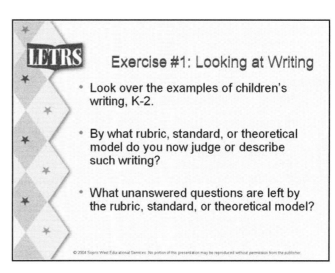

Slide 8

---

[4] Research supporting these conceptualizations is summarized in Berninger, 1994, 1998, 1999; Graham et al., 1996; Graham, 1997; and McCutchen (1996).

FRAMEWORKS TO DESCRIBE THE QUALITY OF CHILDREN'S WRITING		
Stages of the Writing Process	**6+1 Traits Model (Northwest Regional Laboratories)**	**Component Language, Cognitive, and Motor Skills**
Planning/Organization	Ideas	Knowledge of content and the world; memory; imagination
	Organization	Knowledge of genre form and conventions; logical reasoning and use of logical connectors; goal orientation and topic focus
Drafting/ Transcription	Word Choice	Size and depth of vocabulary in lexicon; retrieval and naming ability; access to specific content words; idiomatic and figurative use of language
	Voice	Awareness of audience's needs (perspective taking); self-knowledge and ability to speak with conviction and persuasiveness; pragmatic language ability
	Sentence Fluency	Formulation of complete, varied sentences; compound and complex sentences; grammatical conventions; conventional punctuation and capitalization symbols; letter formation and handwriting fluency; verbal working memory to support online production and monitoring of output
Revision/ Editing	Conventions	Phonological awareness for phonetic spelling accuracy and self-monitoring of transcription; memory for high frequency word spellings and spelling patterns; knowledge of conventions of grammar and usage; skill at using resources
	Presentation	Spatial organization and design; communicative intent; audience awareness

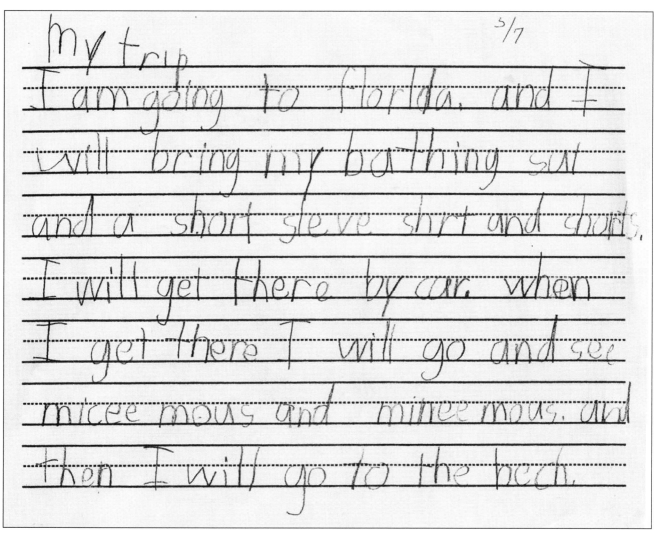

Sample #1: Kindergarten child.

Sample # 1 – "My Trip"

Make observations about:
• Content and Ideas
• Organization
• Word Choice
• Sentences
• Symbolization ("Mechanics") —
  Letter Formation and Spacing,
  Spelling, Punctuation

© 2004 Sopris West Educational Services. No portion of this presentation may be reproduced without permission from the publisher.

Slide 9

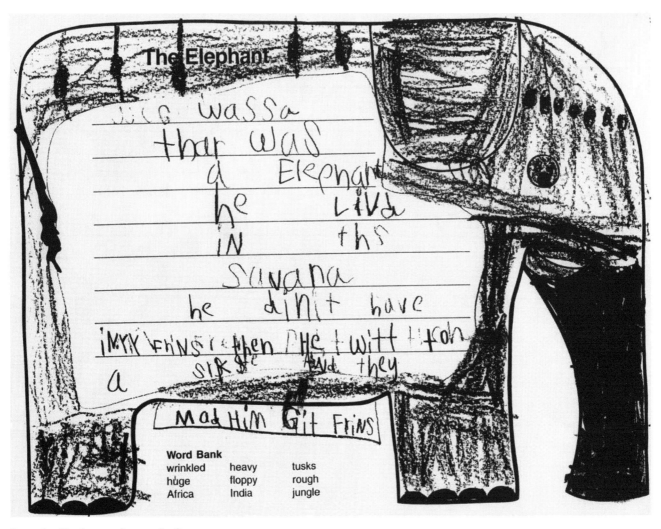

Sample #2: 1st grader, end of year.

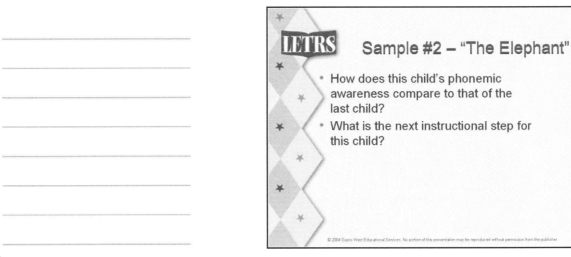

Sample #2 – "The Elephant"

- How does this child's phonemic awareness compare to that of the last child?
- What is the next instructional step for this child?

Siena   May 2,2000

I went in to the Kenthken and
make charchle chip waffife then friend
Nyommie and me Siena. I put the
waffife in the toters. I let it stt
for   15 mintes. Once it's fishe we eat
it.

Bradie   May 7, 2000

I I make ceal for   me. I fix my
own ceal. Then I eet my ceal. It was
good. I do it irvry day.

I make ceal for my friend. He like
ceal to. My friend is nice to me. I'm
nice to him to.

I like to mack Saryow.

fast you got the malie and Saryow
and boln and soon than por the Saryow
and malleck than you ate it.

Sample #3, 4, 5: 2nd graders.

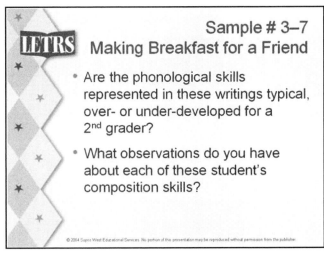

Jasmine   May 1, 2000

FrenchToast

1. first you take the french toats out the bag.
2. Then you git a plate, crup and Parkan buttermilt.
3. Then you put the french Toast in the toaster for 2 mins.
4. Then you git the french toast out the toaster.
5. The you put the french toast on the plate.
6. Then you cut the french toast in half.
7. Then you put the crup on the french toast.
8. Then you and a friend eat the breakfast.

Sample #6: 2nd grader.

Sample # 3–7
Making Breakfast for a Friend

- Are the phonological skills represented in these writings typical, over- or under-developed for a 2nd grader?

- What observations do you have about each of these student's composition skills?

Slide 11

T.   May, 2, 2000.

I would make Frech Toast. First I would get some milk ar... cimmon and bread. Then I would get a pan and stick the bread in the milk and cimmon but you have to make sure that the cimmon does not fall down to the bottom. And if the cimmon falls down stir it up. Put the bread in the bowl and take it out. Let the bread drain and put it in the pan. Cut the stove on. And let it stay on the stove for a little while and then it will be all ready. I learn to cook from watching him.

Sample #7: 2nd grader.

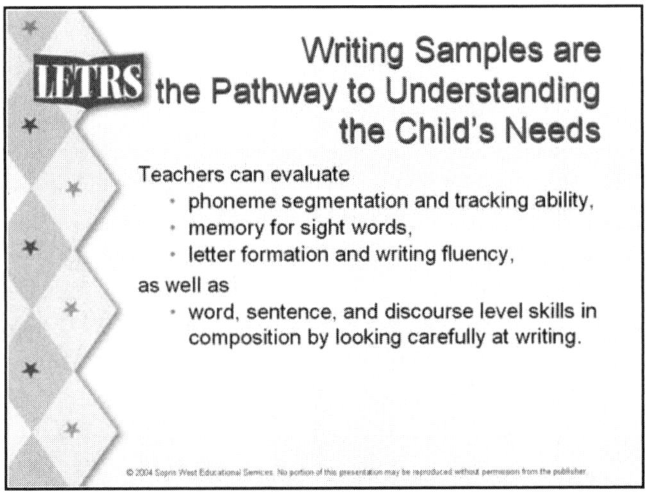

Slide 12

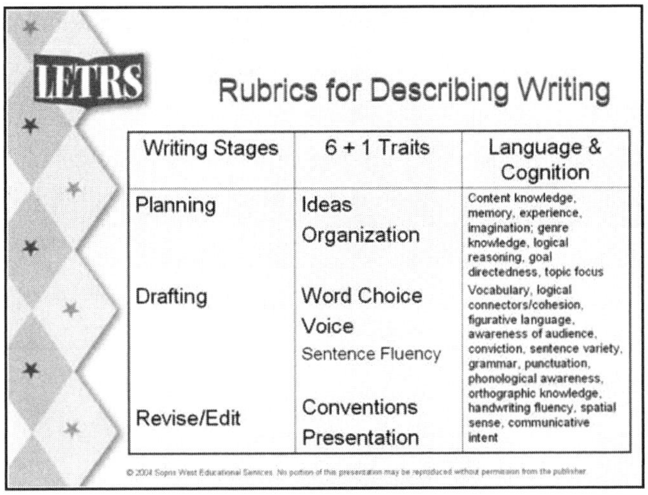

Writing Stages	6 + 1 Traits	Language & Cognition
Planning	Ideas Organization	Content knowledge, memory, experience, imagination; genre knowledge, logical reasoning, goal directedness, topic focus
Drafting	Word Choice Voice Sentence Fluency	Vocabulary, logical connectors/cohesion, figurative language, awareness of audience, conviction, sentence variety, grammar, punctuation, phonological awareness, orthographic knowledge,
Revise/Edit	Conventions Presentation	handwriting fluency, spatial sense, communicative intent

Slide 13

A Closer Look at the Demands of Writing

What Goes Into Planning?

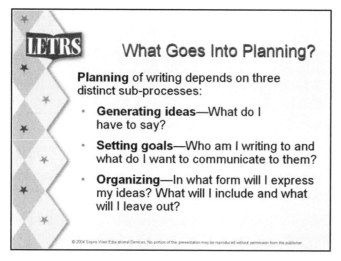

Slide 14

A writer must have a plan or purpose for writing (a **goal**) and access to ideas (an **idea generator**). The writer must be motivated to communicate the ideas with an audience, real or imagined. The ideas must come either from imagination or from experience, immediate or remembered. Thoughts must be ordered in some way (by an executive planner in the mind) that in turn draws on previous knowledge of text organization, strategies for crafting the piece, or stated needs of an audience.

As beginners, children often wonder if they have ideas to express when they are faced with having to write. While some children are highly verbal and confident in self-expression, others "draw a blank" and have difficulty formulating thoughts about a topic. Having something to say can be a major dilemma for a young child, especially one with a limited vocabulary or limited expressive language skill. Furthermore, children usually know that writing is not simply speech written down, and the inherent demands of the task may further inhibit their ability to express ideas. Thus, many children need structure and supportive aids or strategies such as the following:

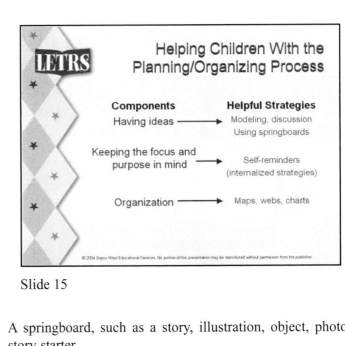

Slide 15

♦ A springboard, such as a story, illustration, object, photograph, or story starter

♦ Thorough exploration of background information about a topic before the child is asked to write about it

♦ A model of the kind of writing that is requested so that imitation or paraphrase of the model is possible

♦ A list of ideas about a topic, and verbal, graphic, or pictorial representation of the ideas that the writing will entail

♦ An organizational plan, such as a story frame, semantic web, sequence chart, or main idea—supporting details outline

♦ Self-instruction strategies, such as remembering to ask oneself who is going to read the writing, and remembering to check if the words are on the topic and goal is being achieved

As children progress in writing development beyond the primary grades, greater independence in topic choice, topic elaboration, and organization is likely if the basic foundations that support writing fluency are established.

 In your experience, what kind of "springboards" have first or second grade children responded well to?

What Goes Into Translating or Drafting?

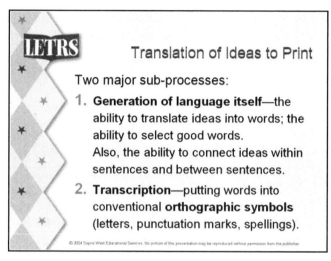

Slide 16

After conjuring up or generating ideas, the writer must formulate or select words and phrases to express those ideas, via a mental "**text generator**," as composing takes place. Words and sentences must then be held in working memory long enough to be **transcribed** into written text. The transcription process calls on sensory systems, grapho-motor skills such as sequential and coordinated finger movements and memory for letter formation, phoneme-grapheme associations for spelling, orthographic memory for letter sequences in words, and memory for punctuation symbols.

These transcription processes employ sensory-motor feedback systems but are regulated by attention and executive systems. The functional processing systems are connected in the language centers of the brain. If transcription (spelling and handwriting) is automatized or accomplished without undue effort and attention, posterior (back) brain systems and lower level brain systems execute and monitor the production of text. If transcription processes are effortful and non-automatic, the writer is using up valuable attention capacity in working memory to get the letters and words on the page. If transcription demands much attention and effort, then less attention is available for generating the text or keeping track of the writer's goals.

Beginning writing instruction must help young children develop habits and skills of transcription. Children can gain command of accurate and fluent handwriting, spelling, and sentence production even while they are asked to have ideas, organize them, and get them on paper. Young children may need considerable assistance to find the words they want, and a number of strategies can keep them from "blocking" as they start to write. These include:

♦ Talking out ideas before writing them down.

♦ Having a list of topic words available.

♦ Looking at a word bank for commonly used words.

♦ Working within a format or framework in which many words are supplied already.

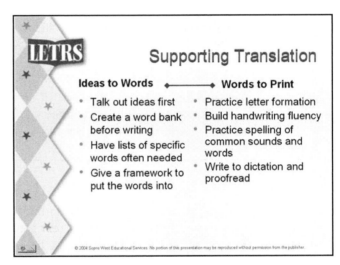

Slide 17

The translation of ideas into words (text generation) depends on the ability to retrieve and select words and to formulate sentences. Choosing words requires access to a sufficiently large working vocabulary, and if children lack words, they may write very little or reuse a few words repeatedly. The choice of words to express ideas during composing necessitates having a well-stocked mental dictionary.

In summary, the translation component of writing is the one that most dramatically distinguishes the competence of children from that of adults. Children's writing fluency and writing quality will depend on getting foundation skills under the pen, as it were, so that attention can be directed toward composing.

 Have you known children who seem to have specific problems with either "text generation" or "transcription" during the drafting stage of writing?

What Goes Into Review and Revision?

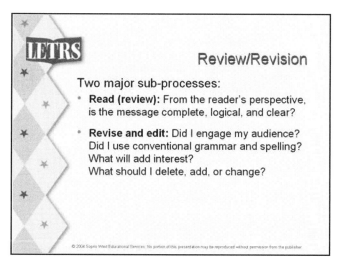

Slide 18

Review and **revision** occur during the generation of text and after the generation of text. Polishing a writing product before publication is a never-ending task for even accomplished authors. Review is the process of looking as objectively as possible at one's own work from the perspective of the reader. The reader needs conventional transcription of language and clarity of expression. Revision of a draft may occur at every level: word choice, sentence structure, overall organization, elaboration or deletion of ideas, and the print symbols themselves.

Young children learning to write are often resistant to revising a written product. They want it over and done, and then they want to move on. If the written product itself is generated with great effort, because transcription skills are not yet well-developed or automatized, children want to protect their work. As the brain matures and skill develops, children attain the cognitive perspective to evaluate their own writing from the point of view of someone who reads it. Awareness of audience can be cultivated in middle grade students through direct strategy instruction[5] but young children may simply grow from sharing their writing with others who have a chance to react to it. As young writers mature, their cognitive systems can handle with increasing flexibility the jobs of monitoring what is being written and what has been written. They can think about the goal they began with even as they are writing. As writers have more words to draw on, more fluency with sentences, and more knowledge of writing conventions, a draft can be compared to an inwardly held standard.

[5] See Graham (1997) for summaries of research on the usefulness of self-instructional writing strategies.

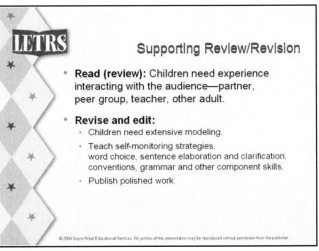

Slide 19

The more perfunctory demand of revision is proofreading for grammar, punctuation, capitalization, and spelling. Obviously, in order to proofread, the child must have established solid skills in each of these areas. The incidental practice that comes from proofreading one's own work is not sufficient for many children to learn each of the important conventions of language and symbolization in writing. Children benefit from experiences sharing their work with their peers and other audiences, as long as the commentary is supportive and focused on content. Revision is learned in small steps, with frequent modeling on the part of the instructor.

Teaching writing is complex because higher level and lower level skills must be taught. Skills must be developed to an automatic level so that the mind has the attention available to think about the audience, the topic, the organization of the piece, and the words that are chosen to express ideas. Even capable children need a high degree of structure and support in the beginning stages of writing.

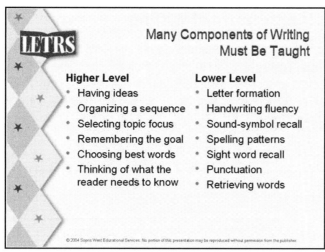

Slide 20

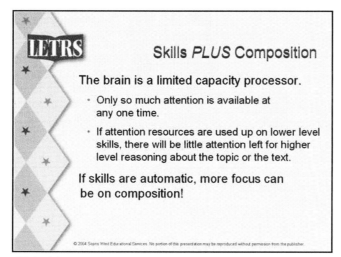

Slide 21

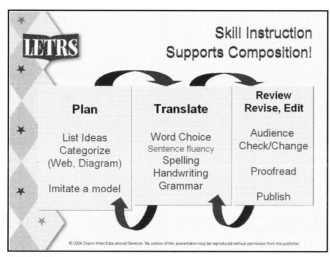

Slide 22

The Whole Enterprise of Writing

As the following schematic diagram shows, writing calls on more cognitive, linguistic, and sensory-motor resources than reading, speaking, or listening. These resources are tapped in an interactive, cyclical manner during skilled writing. Novice writers, however, acquire mastery over the components gradually, a few at a time.

Exercise #2: Summarize the Complexity of Writing

Write a paragraph that expresses why writing is the most demanding language skill and why it is important for educators to appreciate the complexity of skilled writing. Before you write your summary, study the model on the next page. Volunteers may be asked to share what they have written.

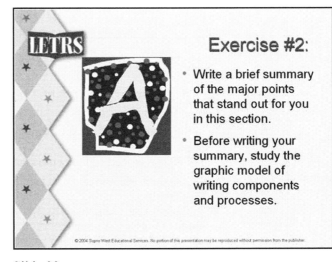

Slide 23

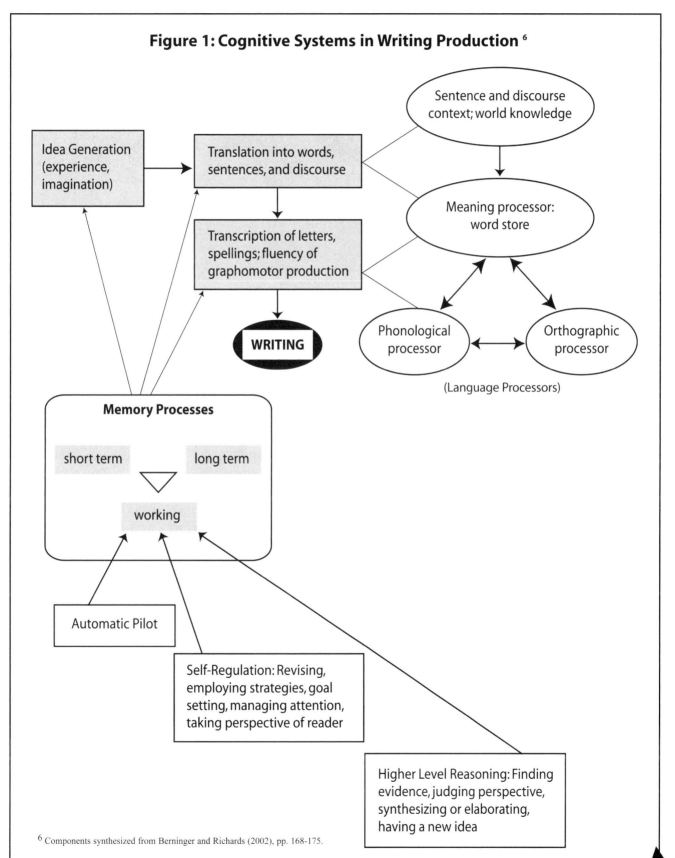

Figure 1: Cognitive Systems in Writing Production [6]

[6] Components synthesized from Berninger and Richards (2002), pp. 168-175.

The Special Characteristics of Written Language

Exercise #3: What's Special About the Language We Write?	
Words	
Phrases and Expressions	
Sentences	
Context for use	
Structure of text	
Purpose	

© 2004 Sopris West Educational Services. No portion of this presentation may be reproduced without permission from the publisher.

Slide 24

Learning to compose is not the inverse of learning to read or talk. The language of conversation is characterized by face-to-face feedback and turn-taking between the speakers. The manner of speaking, the words one chooses, the tone of voice and gestures—all are part of a code that is shared between speakers in the context of the exchange. The style of communication varies according to the speakers' relationships. The way language is used among individuals is one important signal of group membership and social organization. We speak one way with a friend, another way with a child, another way with a respected elder. One can take liberties in conversation with word choice, grammar, and sentence structure (or lack of sentence structure!) that are not permitted in written expression. Our capacity to speak many different forms of our first language, depending on the situational context, is a fascinating topic of pragmatics.

Academic discourse—the conventional language of writing—is a unique form of language with special structures, conventions, and content that must be learned gradually over many years.

© The New Yorker Collection 1986 by Richard Cline. Reprinted with permission.

"Why am I talking this loud?
Because I'm wrong."

Exercise #3: What's Distinctive About Written Language

What is distinctive about language we write? What is distinctive about the communicative relationship between writer and reader? Spend a few minutes listing as many specific linguistic requirements and constraints of formal, conventional written language (academic discourse) as you can.

Level of Language	Written Language	Conversational Speech
Sounds		
Words		
Sentences		
Paragraphs		
Conventions		

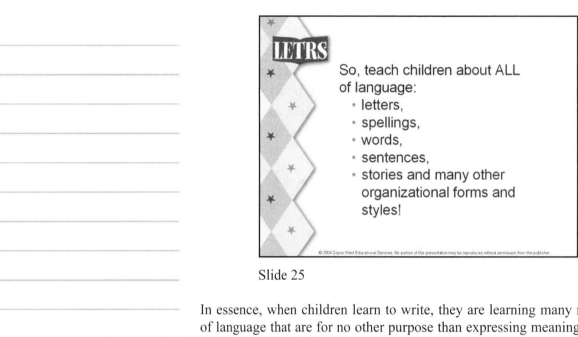

Slide 25

In essence, when children learn to write, they are learning many new forms of language that are for no other purpose than expressing meaning clearly in print. Next, we will focus on the skills that must be taught to young writers in the classroom:

- ◆ Letter formation

- ◆ Alphabet knowledge

- ◆ Sound-symbol correspondence

- ◆ Spelling and word study

- ◆ Handwriting fluency

- ◆ Sentence composition

- ◆ Linking sentences into paragraphs

Finally, we will review the stages of the writing process and how to provide structure and guidance to young children who are just learning to grapple with the demands of writing.

On to Writing Instruction

The most common characteristic of poor or novice writing is its brevity and sparseness. Children may list ideas, often in an unconnected manner, without sufficient elaboration. Sparse communication of ideas, however, is closely associated with problematic vocabulary, grammar, spelling, punctuation, capitalization, and handwriting. Effective instruction must build basic skills in less able and very young writers, even while it provides practice with purposeful, meaningful written communication.

Letter Formation

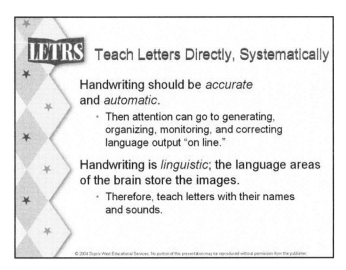

Slide 26

According to Abbott and Berninger (1993), children who have trouble with handwriting are demonstrating more than just a hand-eye coordination problem. Letters are codes for speech sounds that are processed and stored in the language centers of the brain. Dyslexic students with severe reading and spelling problems often have trouble with letter formation, even though they may be well coordinated in other ways, because they have difficulty with many aspects of language symbolization.

The goal of handwriting instruction is the development of grapho-motor habits—smooth sequences of pencil strokes for each letter, made in a specific direction, with size relative to other letters. Sensory feedback and timing are involved in directing the hand. Letter formation becomes automatic when the component strokes are executed accurately without conscious planning. Again, fluent letter formation facilitates composition. Try to write the new letter you see on the slide.

Slide 27

Write the new symbol here:

_____

_____

_____

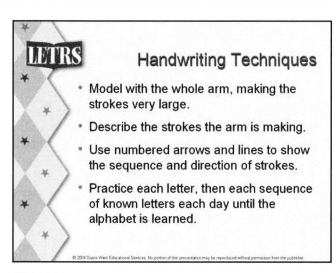

Slide 28

Experience Dysgraphia

- Write a sentence with your non-dominant hand. How does that feel?
- Time yourself to see how long it takes to write the alphabet with each hand.
- Satisfactory writing fluency means producing the cursive alphabet in 20–30 seconds MAX

  (Ray Beck et al.).

- Are you fluent?

© 2004 Sopris West Educational Services. No portion of this presentation may be reproduced without permission from the publisher.

Slide 29

Now, write the alphabet (manuscript or cursive or both) here with your non-dominant hand:

_____

_____

_____

Spelling

Accurate and automatic spelling of patterns and words also supports fluent writing. Spelling is much harder than word recognition in reading. To spell a word, one must know all of its letters, whereas to read a word, one can recognize it with an incomplete memory of the letter sequence. The spellings for sounds (250+) are more numerous and varied than the sounds for spellings (44). Furthermore, spelling recall depends on knowledge of morphemes and syllable patterns.

What is known about effective spelling instruction? It must be at the right level of challenge for the child, and it should teach sounds, symbols, syllables, morphemes, memory techniques, information about the history of our language, and self-monitoring strategies.[7] We remember best what makes sense to us, and spelling (yes, even English) can be made to make sense.

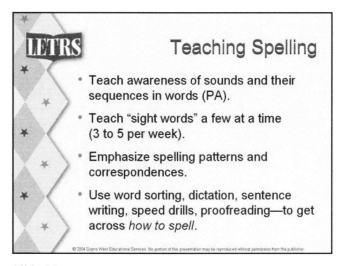

Slide 30

---

[7] These concepts and the structure of the orthography are explored in depth in Modules 1 to 3 of *LETRS*.

For a taste of a "word study" approach to spelling instruction, try sorting the words on the slide into three categories. Then, sort the words in each column into two sub-categories. Next, break each word into its base part and its suffix to show what happened when the ending was added. Finally, describe the ending rules that are demonstrated by this activity.

LETRS Exercise #4: Try a Word Sort

Sort these words into three groups by their endings:

-ed	-ing	-er
penned	winning	fined
dinner	diner	cloned
humming	perfumed	donned
thinner	assuming	stoning
whiner	stemming	

© 2004 Sopris West Educational Services. No portion of this presentation may be reproduced without permission from the publisher.

Slide 31

Exercise #4: Word Sort for Word Study

–ed	–ing	–er

(continued) **Exercise #4:** Word Sort for Word Study

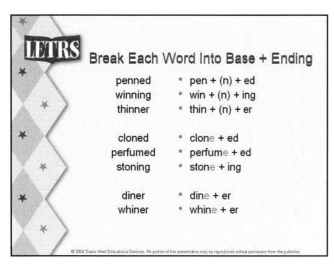

**Exercise #4:
Sort Each Column Again**

penned	winning	dinner
donned	humming	thinner
cloned	stemming	diner
perfumed	stoning	whiner
fined	assuming	

© 2004 Sopris West Educational Services. No portion of this presentation may be reproduced without permission from the publisher.

Slide 32

Break Each Word Into Base + Ending

penned	° pen + (n) + ed
winning	° win + (n) + ing
thinner	° thin + (n) + er
cloned	° clone + ed
perfumed	° perfume + ed
stoning	° stone + ing
diner	° dine + er
whiner	° whine + er

© 2004 Sopris West Educational Services. No portion of this presentation may be reproduced without permission from the publisher.

Slide 33

(continued) **Exercise #4:** Word Sort for Word Study

What spelling rule does each word show? List the words.			
No change	**Doubling**	**Change y to i**	**Drop silent –e**

Analyze and explain what is happening when certain suffixes and inflections are added to base words.

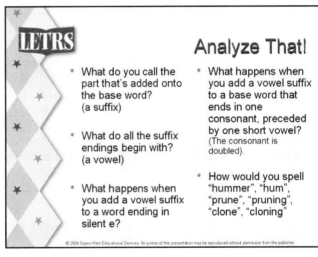

Slide 34

Fluency in Component Skills

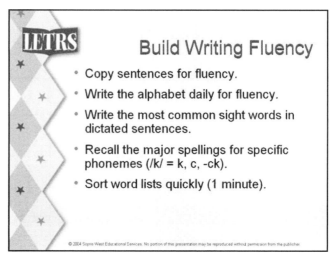

Slide 35

Berninger and her colleagues have published multiple studies showing that brief fluency drills in writing have a beneficial effect similar to that of fluency drills in reading: They support the child's ability to focus on the higher purposes and more challenging aspects of composition, because the "lower level" skills are accurate and automatic.

Thus, writing lessons can include "warm-ups"—exercises for the hand and the mind. For about five minutes, students practice the basics—letter formation, sentence copying, word spellings, sentence completion, or the alphabet. Drills should be brief, frequent, and varied—and they are never the whole lesson.

Sentence Writing

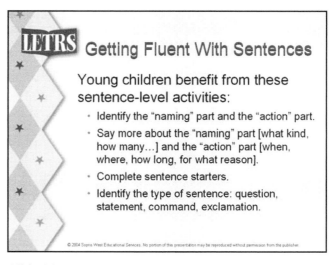

Slide 36

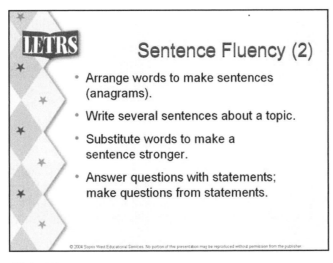

Slide 37

Formulation of sentences is expected of children from first grade on, but children with language limitations may not have a well-developed sense of what is meant by "sentence." A sentence is not simply "a group of words with a capital and period." Children need ways to think about an ungrammatical, incomplete, or run-on sentence so that they can fix it.

Direct teaching of sentence form is a necessity for young writers. A system of marking sentence parts, identifying the grammatical role of words, and expanding sentences systematically should be used and practiced. At the first and second grade level, emphasize what each of the sentence parts does before introducing formal grammatical terms.[8]

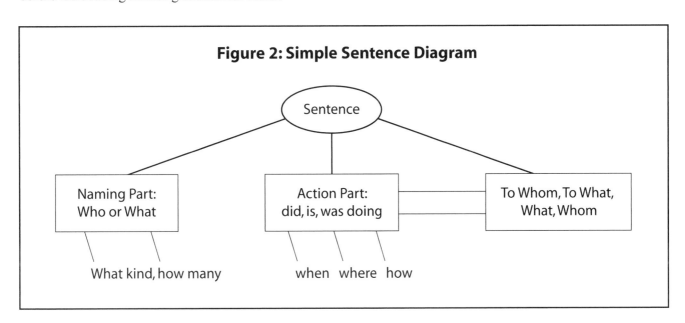

Figure 2: Simple Sentence Diagram

Sentence

Naming Part: Who or What — What kind, how many

Action Part: did, is, was doing — when where how

To Whom, To What, What, Whom

---

[8] Building sentences with categories of words is traditional methodology with children who need a structured approach. See *Framing Your Thoughts* (T. Greene and M.E. Enfield, 1993; Language Circle Enterprises, Bloomington, MN), and the *Fokes Sentence Builder* (J. Fokes, 1976, Teaching Resources).

Daily sentence manipulations help children develop writing fluency and include such activities as:

- ◆ Expand simple sentences in response to questions who, what, when, why, and how.

- ◆ Make sentences with several given words.

- ◆ Start sentences with unusual words.

- ◆ Select specific nouns and strong verbs for simple sentences.

- ◆ Identify the subject (who, what) and predicate (is doing) of each sentence, using single and double underlines.

- ◆ Label the grammatical role of words with index cards or color codes for each category. Formal terminology (noun, verb) can be delayed until children know the categories by function (who, did what, to whom, where, and so forth).

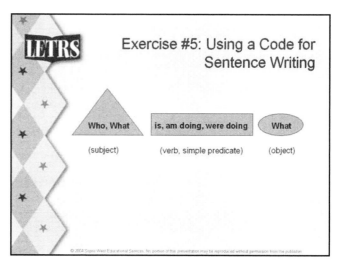

Slide 38

Teaching Beginning Spelling and Writing

Exercise #5: Using a Code for Sentence Writing

Using this code, create sentences that follow each pattern.

Who, what   Is, am doing, was doing

Example: Zack digs.

_____

_____

Who, what   Is, am doing, was doing   What (object)

Example: Zack digs the hole.

_____

_____

Who, what **+** Who, what   Is, am doing, was doing **+** Is, am doing, was doing   What

Example: Zack and Zeke are digging and uncovering old bones.

_____

_____

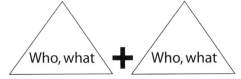

Who, what   Is, am/was doing   What   Joining word   Who, what   Is, am/was doing   What

Example: Zack dug old bones while Zeke prepared the display.

_____ (but) _____

_____ (although) _____

Linkage of sentences with connecting words and references is required if children are to give their compositions cohesion or wholeness. Adult writers accomplish linkage through devices such as repeating a reference to the topic, using pronouns, and using signal and connecting words of various kinds. The relationships among ideas or propositions in the sentences is signaled explicitly by specific vocabulary.

Children gradually develop an understanding of logical relationships referred to by connection words. According to Jacobs (1997), children understand the concept of conjunction (and, both) by second grade. Not until sixth grade, however, do they fully understand disjunction between propositions or ideas (but, or, either-or). Conditionality (if-then; if and only if) continues to be learned into eleventh grade. In the early stages of language learning, children show connection simply by proximity—that is, putting sentences next to each other. Next, they learn to use "and" for a number of meanings, including addition, time, cause, and condition. Next comes the use of conditional terms such as "when," "because," "unless," and "if," used by most children in their oral language by the time they enter school.

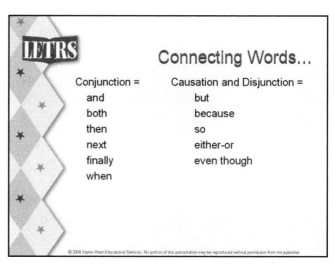

Slide 39

Progression of Children's Use of Coordinate and Subordinate Conjunctions

1 Conjunction and Sequence	2 Causation	3 Disjunction and Alternation	4 Conditionality
and both then when	because so	but or either-or neither-nor even though	unless although if if-then if only

Children's writing growth recapitulates their oral language growth; the first connective to be used for multiple purposes is "and." In low-income second graders, Jacobs found that the repertoire for connective words included those for addition (*and*); time (*and, then, when*); and, to a lesser extent, causal relationships (*because, so*). Children a year older signaled disjunction (*but*) and the manner of action (*like, how*). At grade 4 and up, logical relationships expressed in connecting words included alternation (*or*), general to specific (*for example*), and concession (*even though*).

These data, then, suggest that children may benefit from:

♦ Direct teaching about words that connect ideas within and between sentences

♦ Practice using those words to connect simple sentences or elaborate the ideas in sentences

♦ Practice constructing compound and complex sentence forms in which cause and effect, conditionality, or subordination are expressed

What Should a Teacher Expect of Developing Writers?

Slide 40

Children typically know the distinguishing features of orthography from age 2 or 3. Even by that age, they know that writing differs from drawing in several ways: writing conveys a message, is produced in a direction across the page (in English), has distinct letter forms, and is read back.

By kindergarten (age 5), children typically know at least a few letter forms, that spaces are between words, that writing goes left to right, and that print is organized from top to bottom on a page. They may attempt to write messages of their own and read them back. They may or may not know the alphabetic principle—that alphabet letters represent the speech sounds in words—and be able to produce early phonetic spellings that represent some of the salient sounds in a word.

By first grade, most children are either early phonetic or later phonetic writers. They spell by sound, using alphabet letter names and literal phonetic transcriptions of what they hear and feel as they say a word. They work hard at forming letters if the motor patterns are taught. They begin to write words in sequence, with word spaces and periods at the ends of sentences. They remember the spellings of commonly used sight words if practice and exposure is sufficient. Depending on the emphasis of instruction and the ability of the learner, this stage proceeds more or less quickly.

By second grade, basic transcription skills should be well enough established that children can attend more readily to the demands of composition. Children in second grade may be somewhat amenable to revision especially in response to conferences with peers and adults about their writing. Children in second grade should start to adjust their approach to writing according to the requirements of the task—whether it is a story, an explanation, a poem, or a description. More planning and more independence in generating ideas should be expected. Linking sentences together in a basic paragraph should be a goal at this stage.

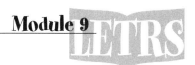
Exercise #6: Writing Skill in Various First Graders

Look at the following writing samples from first grade children who have been assessed with the Dynamic Indicators of Basic Early Literacy Skills (DIBELS) and who are in grades K–2. In what way do the words, sentences, and overall quality of language and ideas correspond to the children's status as "low risk," "some risk," and "at risk"?

Case #1, C.P.

First grader, early January composition. Low risk on DIBELS measures, doing extremely well in letter naming (99th percentile), phoneme segmentation (99th percentile), nonsense word reading (98th percentile) and word use fluency (76th percentile).

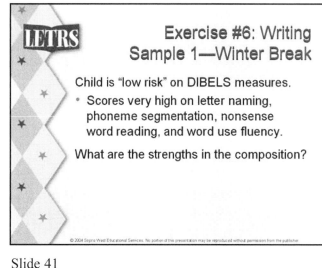

Slide 41

1-10-02

To begin with I watched my Harry Potter movie. It was exiting! My favorite part was when they whire *were* playing cheos. *chess.* The movie It has never befor seen *had* footadge at the end. Then We opened presents and I got lots cool prdrumset form *from* my brother. I played with it

evry day but my dad *accidently* ntly broak it. *broke it!* We can't fix it and I don't like it at all. Brut I still play it. *consequently* me and my brother played catch. It was very, very, very fun! We played it all day then we went inside to have dinner. Latter, we

As you can see my Winter Vacation was very, very fun.

(continued) **Exercise #6:** Writing Skill in Various First Graders

Case #2, N.C.

First grader, early December composition. At some risk on DIBELS measures: 64th percentile on letter naming, 15th percentile on phoneme segmentation; 21st percentile on nonsense word reading; 44th percentile on word use fluency. Receives ½ hour per day extra small group help with multisensory structured language in addition to classroom *Open Court* program. Also works on CD ROM with Lindamood LIPS Program and Earobics training in phonology.

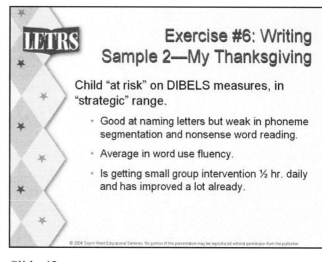

Slide 42

12-7-03

My thankgiving was fun.
Frst thankgiving was a
blast. We had it at
my gramas huse.
We had cake for
luch and it was
good. then after
it was fun at
my cusins huse.
but afder we had to
go home. but
ulee I come
hose with my toys

my favrt food was cake
we had so much
fun do you no
w

(continued) **Exercise #6:** Writing Skill in Various First Graders

Case #3, J.D.

First grader in January. At risk. Needs intensive support. On an IEP since kindergarten; receives one-one tutoring and small group instruction. Letter naming, 21st percentile; phoneme awareness, 4th percentile; nonsense word reading, 31st percentile; word use fluency, 26th percentile.

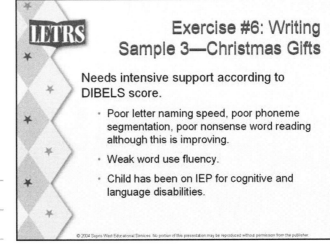

Slide 43

I T A M TRUC (I got a remote control truck).

AED A THTHB (and a chalkboard)

AED A MROED (and a motorcycle guy)

AED A SHPS (and slippers)

AED A FPD (and a leapfrog pad)

1-03

(illegible early-emergent handwriting)

remoten

I got a nemote controll
truck. And a chalkboard
And a motoraycle guy.
And slippers.
And a
Leap frog pad.

(continued) **Exercise #6:** Writing Skill in Various First Graders

Question for discussion:

If these examples are typical, how do they demonstrate the relationship between composition quality, composition fluency, and automatic skill at the level of letter knowledge, letter formation, phoneme awareness, phonics, and vocabulary?

The Writing Process, With Structure

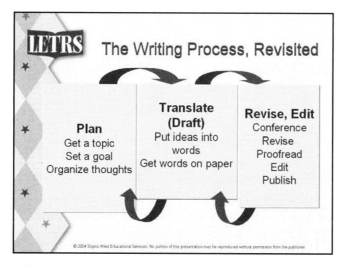

Slide 44

Generate and Organize Ideas Before Writing

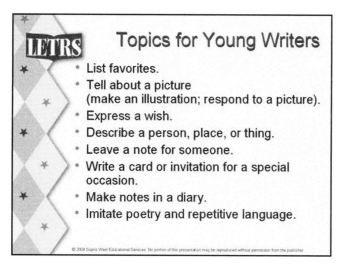

Slide 45

Topics for writing should be offered by the teacher to novice writers for two purposes: to relieve less verbal children from having to generate a topic and to give children experience with different kinds of writing tasks. Most of the writing that children must do from fourth grade on will be academic writing in which they are responding to reading, explaining the answer to a test question, writing a report, or expressing an opinion. Fantasy writing and unstructured writing can be overdone; children need expository writing competence for answering test questions and generating summaries, explanations, requests, and comparisons. Give a variety of topics. "Knowledge telling" is the level at which beginners can be successful (Scardamalia and Bereiter, 1986).

Show the children a model of what is expected, or walk them through a "shared writing" in which a model is generated by the class together. Help the children conceptualize or visualize the end product they are striving to create. Give the children a springboard to jump from:

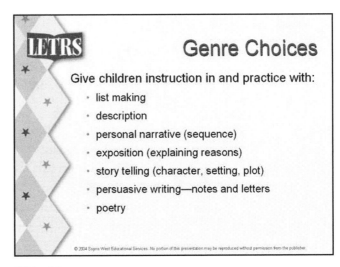

Slide 46

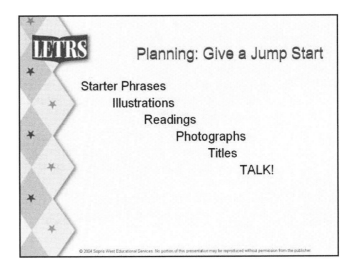

Slide 47

◆ Read about a topic or share an experience organized around a topic before expecting children to write about it.

◆ Collect key vocabulary about the topic and post it.

◆ Put key vocabulary on "bookmarks" children can refer to as they write.

◆ Use visual prompts such as photographs, paintings, sculpture, or curious objects to stimulate ideas.

◆ Use questions who, what, where, when, how, why to help children elaborate ideas.

◆ Explicitly talk about the thought processes that go into word selection and sentence formation as you write down the children's ideas.

◆ Identify the audience and the purpose for writing.

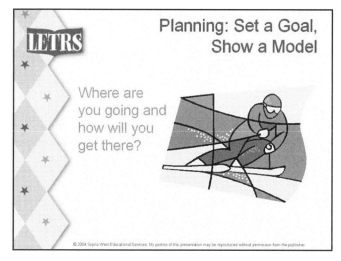

Slide 48

◆ Take the ideas that have been generated and ask the children to organize them. Use a simple story structure for narrative writing, and a simple paragraph format for expository writing.

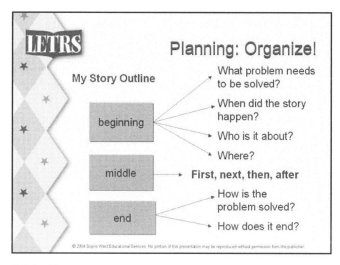

Slide 49

Composing a Draft

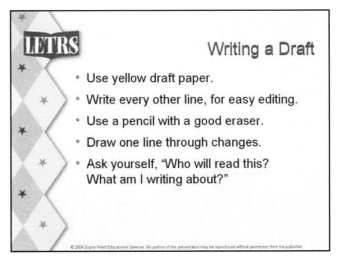

Slide 50

As children write a draft, be sure they are referring to the brainstorming and organizational plan they just completed. State from the outset that drafts can always be improved and that good writers revisit their work many times to revise, edit, and polish.

♦ Use lined, yellow paper. Encourage students to leave a space between each line so editing will be easier.

♦ Give words to begin the composition or give children lists or templates to complete if they are slow to generate words themselves.

♦ Vary the expectations for students; listing is a beginning skill, sentence writing more advanced, and organized linking of sentences into paragraphs is the most challenging.

♦ (Late first or second grade) Give a template for a simple paragraph; model paragraph construction many times (topic sentence, supporting details, closing sentence).

Review and Revision

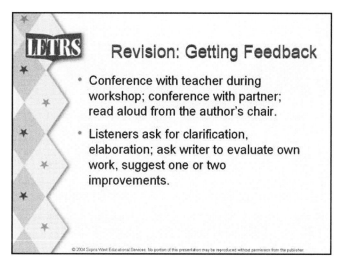

Slide 51

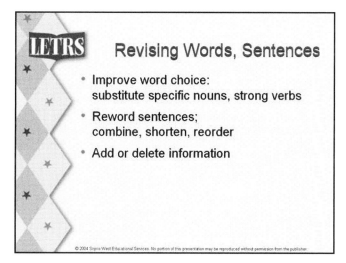

Slide 52

◆ Keep an Author's Chair for students to occupy while they share their writing; ask a few students daily to read their work aloud and take suggestions.

◆ Read incomplete sentences aloud and ask children if they sound right. Create a complete sentence from the fragment.

◆ Select two or three sentences from the children's work, write them on a chart or chalkboard, and proofread together with the class. Use these to remind the class about skills already taught and practiced. Focus children on word choice, especially the subject noun and main verb. Look for opportunities to combine simple sentences into a compound or complex sentence.

◆ Keep personal proofreading checklists on bookmarks or in folders. Limit the number of corrections students are expected to make on their own.

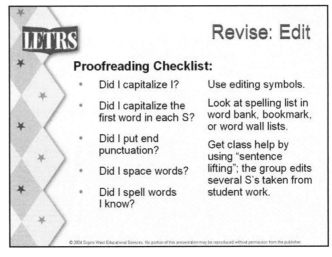

Slide 53

◆ Supervise peer feedback sessions; set ground rules for students to comment on each other's work. The writer holds on to the work and keeps control of it.

Questions to an author after hearing the draft:

I liked the part where you said _____.

I thought the best words you used were _____.

Which part do you like? _____?

I wish you said a lot more about _____.

Did you think about something that you want to add _____?

Publishing

Slide 54

♦ Post corrected and neatly presented work to share with a larger audience.

♦ Find real audiences who will read the writing.

♦ Keep each child's writing in a personal writing folder. It is easy to see progress over the year.

A Lesson Format, Grades 1 and 2

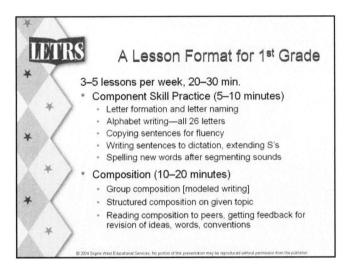

Slide 55

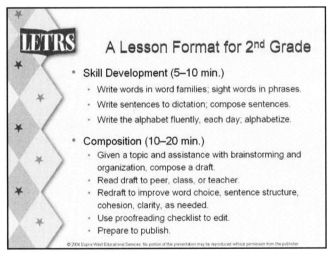

Slide 56

(continued) **A Lesson Format, Grades 1 and 2**

5-Minute Warm-Up: Practice and Build Transcription Fluency
- Form a few letters, using numbered arrow cues, tracing, verbalizing, writing from memory, and evaluating accuracy.
- Produce the alphabet, in sequence, one or two times per session, until fluency is achieved.
- Write graphemes learned for sounds (vowels and consonants), including letter combinations such as vowel teams and digraphs.
- Combine onsets and rimes to write whole syllables.
- Write high frequency words to dictation, a few at a time singly or in sentences; say the letters as a word is written.

10–20 Minutes: Compose With Teacher Modeling and Assistance
Planning
- Establish the goal of the activity.
- Establish the topic.
- Show a model of a finished product.
- Build or elicit topic knowledge from students.
- Generate ideas for writing and list them.
- Help students arrange ideas in order.

Drafting (Transcribing)
- Compose in dialogue with the students and write down what they say on a chart, overhead, or cue cards.
- Begin sentences with the students and have them complete the sentences.
- Encourage students to prompt themselves with self-talk.

Review and Revision (as appropriate after conferences)
- Students share writing with peers or adults.
- Talk over what can be added, deleted, elaborated, or rearranged.
- Lift one or two sentences from children's work to demonstrate proofreading and editing.
- Give children an individualized proofreading checklist to find and correct spelling, grammar, punctuation, capitalization, and usage that they have been taught.

Exercise #7: Let's Write!

Here are four different writing assignments that can be generated after students read the story, *A Home for Lizzie*. Try each one. Have fun!

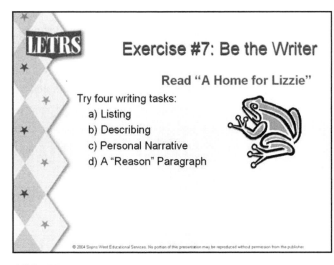

Slide 57

(continued) **Exercise #7:** Let's Write!

I. **Lists and Categories**

Backyard Discoveries (Brainstorm)—What surprises have you found in your backyard or the neighborhood around your house?

Now, let's put your discoveries into categories. If you find something new today or tomorrow, we'll decide what category it goes in . . . and add it to our list!

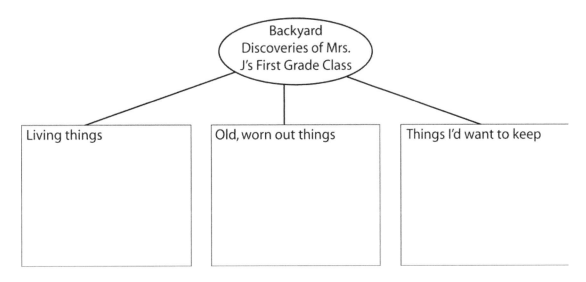

(continued) **Exercise #7:** Let's Write!

II. **Description: My Favorite Place to Be**

Today, class, we will be thinking about our favorite place to be and finding good words that describe how that place feels, looks, sounds, and smells, and why we like to be there.

My favorite place to be is on my couch, in front of my fireplace, at home with a good book in the evening. It's quiet and peaceful. I feel safe, relaxed, and content there. What's your favorite place? Call on some volunteers. Remind them to tell you words that describe feelings, sights, sounds, smells, and actions going on in that place.

I feel	I see	I hear	I taste	I do	I smell

Now, write some sentences about your favorite place. You can use these for starters if you like, or you can make your own sentences:

My favorite place to be is_____.

When I am there I like to _____.

I go there (when) _____.

I feel _____._____ I hear

_____.

I see _____. It's my favorite place!

When you are ready, find a partner and share what you have written. Let your partner ask you three questions about your favorite place. Then see if there is anything else you would like to add to your description.

(continued) **Exercise #7:** Let's Write!

III. **A Personal Narrative**

The little girl in our story (*A Home for Lizzie*) found a creature in her backyard. At first she wanted to keep it. Then she realized that the creature was happier and more likely to live if she let it go.

Have you ever found something that you decided to let go or give back? Do you remember what made you decide to let it go or give it back? Do you remember how you felt about that? Tell what you did and what happened. First, talk about your idea with a partner. Then, plan the parts of your personal narrative.

Title or Topic

Beginning (where, when, who) "One day ..."

What problem needs to be solved?

Events that happened (first, then, next, finally)

How the story ends. How is the problem resolved?

Now, write your story on another piece of paper! Remember to leave space between the lines and write in pencil.

(continued) **Exercise #7:** Let's Write!

IV. **Organized Paragraph That Explains Reasons for Something**

I'm going to show you a way to think about the jobs of each of the sentences in a paragraph. When we write a paragraph that explains the reasons why we want something or why some-thing is true, that paragraph begins with a topic sentence. We'll code that sentence blue because it is the overarching "sky" sentence under which everything else goes.

(blue) Public parks are an important part of our town.

Next, we want to add another sentence that restates and explains the topic sentence further. This will be the green sentence because it has some blue in it but it adds a little more information.

(green) Without parks, both people and animals would have less space for necessities.

Next we want to add some details or some reasons why the first sentences are true. We want to tell the reader more about this topic and explain why [parks are important]. We'll code these sentences yellow because they shine light on the topic.

(yellow) Without parks, many birds would have no homes.
Parks are our play space.
Parks add beauty to the city.

These sentences still need some flesh or some meat. We'll add even more detail under each one, and code those sentences red—the meat on the bones!

(yellow) Without parks, many birds would have no homes. **(red)** They need trees to nest and grass to put in the nests. **(yellow)** Parks are our play space. **(red)** Where else can we find a swing set or place to skateboard? **(yellow)** Parks also add beauty to the city. **(red)** I'd rather look at grass and trees than at concrete all the time. **(blue)** Public parks are worth every cent that the city spends on them.

(continued) **Exercise #7:** Let's Write!

At the end, we added a blue-green sentence: It has some of the topic sentence in it but the words are not exactly the same. We have wrapped up the paragraph by restating the main idea in different words. Now, here's our paragraph:

> Public parks are an important part of our town. Without parks, both people and animals would have less space for necessities. Without parks, many birds would have no homes. They need trees to nest and grass to put in the nests. Parks are our play space. Where else can we find a swing set or place to skateboard? Parks also add beauty to the city. I'd rather look at grass and trees than at concrete all the time. Public parks are worth every cent that the city spends on them.

Now, let's go back and put in some polish. We can add transition words that connect the ideas and change some words to make the sentences sound better.

> Public parks are an important part of our town. Without parks, both people and animals would have less space for necessities. For example, many birds would have no homes. Birds of many kinds need trees to build nests and grass for lining the nests. Parks are also the space where people and dogs can play. Where else can we find a swing set, place to skateboard, or place to take a pet? Finally, parks add beauty to the city. I'd rather look at grass and trees than at concrete all the time, wouldn't you? Public parks are worth every cent that the city spends on them.

NOW, YOU WRITE! As you make your structured paragraph, use your markers to indicate what kind of sentence you are composing (topic, elaboration, reason/detail, more meat, conclusion).

Summary

Summary Points From
Writing Research

- Children may be good at generating words orally but may have significant problems with handwriting or spelling.

- Children may be good at handwriting or spelling and have trouble generating ideas, organizing, elaborating, or revising written work.

© 2004 Sopris West Educational Services. No portion of this presentation may be reproduced without permission from the publisher.

Slide 58

Summary Points From Writing
Research (2)

- Children with spelling problems write fewer words.
- Handwriting problems are associated with lower quality of composition.
- Handwriting and spelling account for 66% of the variance in primary grade writing fluency (words per minute).

(Berninger, 1999)

© 2004 Sopris West Educational Services. No portion of this presentation may be reproduced without permission from the publisher.

Slide 59

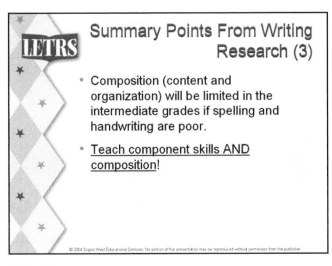

Slide 60

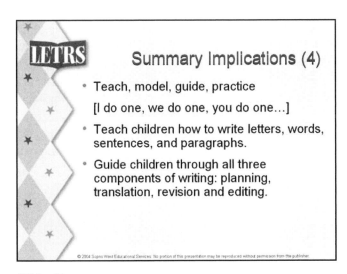

Slide 61

Building a "writing brain," according to Berninger and Richards (2002) to support writing means building a proficient language system from all functional components. All the mental and linguistic processors that support listening, speaking, and reading are employed in writing, with the addition of other sensory, motor, attention, memory, and executive functions. Working memory is heavily taxed during writing. The "juggling act" is daunting: One must hold in mind what one wants to say, recall specific symbolic forms, keep the goal and organization in mind, and monitor whether the writing is communicating to the reader.

Working memory, however, is a limited capacity processor. That is, only so much memory is available to devote to any one task. In order to be proficient, the developing writer must automatize skills to free up space for other processes, just as one frees up space on a computer desktop. The conscious mind needs desktop space for all the higher-level problem solving and decision-making that composition demands. As the executive system juggles its various jobs, it is vulnerable to disruption, overload, and faulty processing, especially in the non-expert writer. Children may seem to have learned component skills, such as spelling or paragraphing, but when too many skills are demanded at once during composition the whole system can fail—just as too many appliances plugged into one outlet can cause system overload.

Building a cognitive system that will support writing, therefore, requires strengthening component skills so that they can be used with less attention to each one, increasing "juggling" capacity in the mental desktop, and increasing the repertoire of numerous problem-solving strategies (Scardamalia & Bereiter, 1986).

The primary grades afford an opportunity to teach the most critical skills early and well, and to use structured, supported methods to acquaint children with other writing skills that they will master much later on a developmental continuum. Multiple studies by Berninger, Graham, McCutchen, and others have shown that if the foundations of handwriting, spelling, and sentence fluency are established early, composition quality and length improves in second, third, and fourth grade. Further, failure to establish the skills of transcription compromises the writing development of children whose language skills are otherwise normal. Good transcription ability facilitates composition quality and length.

To teach young children to write, do these things:

- Show them what you want (model).

- Teach handwriting and spelling to the point of automatic and accurate usefulness.

- Teach component skills before requiring their application.

- Give children prompts for ideas and words.

- Show them how to organize before writing.

- Give structure to the draft—as much as is needed.

- Provide an audience response, emphasizing the message in the writing first.

- Provide proofreading and editing assistance.

- Publish in the real world.

Wrap-Up Discussion Questions

1. Why are young children vulnerable to overload during writing? What causes overload?

2. What kinds of tasks, if any, might you want to add to a screening and progress-monitoring assessment of functional writing skills? Are holistic rubrics sufficient for learning what we want to know about developing writers?

3. What is meant by "balance" in an early writing lesson?

4. How can a child who struggles to write be motivated to persist?

Instructional Resources for Multisensory Instruction of Grammar and Beginning Writing

Word Shapes—Carol Stockdale and Carol Possin, Solving Reading Problems, LinguiSystems

Framing Your Thoughts—Project Read, Language Circle Enterprises, Blooomington, Minnesota

Multisensory Grammar—Suzanne Carreker, Neuhaus Center, Houston, TX

Write Well Spelling—Marilyn Sprick, Sopris West, Longmont, CO

Bibliography

Abbott, R., & Berninger, V. (1993). Structural equation modeling of relationships among developmental skills and writing skills in primary and intermediate grade students. *Journal of Educational Psychology, 85,* 478–508.

Allen, K.A., & Beckwith, M.C. (1999). Alphabet knowledge: Letter recognition, naming, and sequencing. In J. Birsh (ed.), *Multisensory Teaching of Basic Language Skills,* (pp. 85–117). Baltimore: Paul Brookes Publishing.

Bain, A. M., Bailet, L. L., & Moats, L.C. (2001). *Written language disorders: Theory into practice.* Austin, TX: Pro-Ed.

Beck, R., Conrad, D., & Anderson, P. (1999). *Basic skill builders.* Longmont, CO: Sopris West Educational Services.

Berninger, V. (1999). Coordinating transcription and text generation in working memory during composing: Automatic and constructive processes. *Learning Disability Quarterly, 22,* 99–112.

Berninger, V. (1998). *Process assessment of the learner: Guides for intervention.* San Antonio, TX: The Psychological Corporation.

Berninger, V. (1994). *Reading and writing acquisition: A developmental neuropsychological perspective.* Madison, WI: WCB Brown & Benchmark.

Berninger, V.W., & Richards, T.L. (2002). *Brain literacy for educators and psychologists.* Amsterdam: Academic Press.

Berninger, V., Vaughn, K., Abbott, R., Brooks, A., Begay, K., Curtis, G., Byrd, K., and Graham, S. (2000). Language-based spelling instruction: Teaching children to make multiple connections between spoken and written words. *Learning Disability Quarterly, 23,* 117–135.

Graham, S. (1997). Executive control in the revising of students with learning and writing difficulties. *Journal of Educational Psychology, 89,* 223–234.

Graham, S., Berninger, V., Abbott, R., Abbott, S., & Whitaker, D. (1996). The role of mechanics in composing of elementary school students: A new methodological approach. *Journal of Educational Psychology, 89,* 170–182.

Harris, K., & Graham, S. (1996). *Making the writing process work: Strategies for composition and self-regulation,* 2nd Edition. Cambridge: Brookline Books.

Hayes, J. R., & Flower, L.S. (1980). Identifying the organization of the writing processes. In L.W. Gregg & E.R. Steinberg (Eds.), *Cognitive processes in writing* (pp. 3–30). Hillsdale, NJ: Erlbaum.

Hillocks, G., Jr. (1986). *Research on written composition: New directions for teaching.* Urbana, IL: National Council for Teachers of English.

Hochman, J. (1999). Teaching written composition. In J. Birsch (Ed.), *Multisensory teaching of basic language skills* (pp. 281–298). Baltimore: Paul Brookes Publishing.

Hooper, S., Swartz, C., Wakely, M., deKruif, R., & Montgomery, J. (2002). Executive functions in elementary school children with and without problems in written expression. *Journal of Learning Disabilites*, *35* (1), 57–68.

Jacobs, V. (1997). The use of connectives in low-income children's writing: Linking reading, writing, and language skill development. In L. Putnam (Ed.), *Readings on language and literacy: Essays in honor of Jeanne S. Chall* (pp. 100–130). Cambridge, MA: Brookline Books.

Myklebust, H. (1973). *Development and disorders of written language: Studies of normal and exceptional children* (Vols. 1–2). New York: Grune & Stratton.

McCutchen, D. (1996). A capacity theory of writing: Working memory in composition. *Educational Psychology Review*, *8*, 299–325.

Moats, L.C. (2000). *Speech to Print: Language essentials for teachers*. Baltimore: Paul Brookes Publishing.

Moats, L.C. (1995). *Spelling: Development, disability, and instruction*. Baltimore: York Press.

National Reading Panel. (2000). *Teaching children to read: An evidence-based assessment of the scientific research literature on reading and its implications for reading instruction.* Washington, DC: National Institute of Child Health and Human Development.

Scardamalia, M., & Bereiter, C. (1986). Research on written composition. In M.C. Wittrock, (Ed.), *Handbook of research on teaching,* 3rd Edition. (pp. 778–803). New York: MacMillan.

Stotsky, S. (2001). Writing: The royal road to reading comprehension. In S. Brody (Ed.), *Teaching reading: Language, letters, and thought* (pp. 276–296). Milford, NH: LARC Publishing.

Tangel, D.M., & Blachman, B.A. (1995). Effect of phoneme awareness instruction on the invented spelling of first grade children: A one-year follow-up. *Journal of Reading Behavior*, *27*, 153–185.

Treiman, R. (1998). Beginning to spell in English. In C. Hulme & R.M. Joshi (Eds.), *Reading and spelling development and disorders*. Mahwah, NJ: Lawrence Erlbaum Associates.

Treiman, R., & Bourassa, D. (2000). The development of spelling skill. *Topics in Language Disorders*, *20*, 1–18.

Uhry, J.K., & Shepherd, M.J. (1993). Segmentation/spelling instruction as part of a first-grade reading program: Effects on several measures of reading. *Reading Research Quarterly*, *28*, 219–233.

Glossary

affix: a morpheme or meaningful part of a word attached before or after a root to modify its meaning; a category that subsumes prefixes, suffixes, and infixes

alphabetic principle: the principle that letters are used to represent individual phonemes in the spoken word; a critical insight for beginning reading and spelling

alphabetic writing system: a system of symbols that represent each consonant and vowel sound in a language

Anglo-Saxon: Old English, a Germanic language spoken in Britain before the invasion of the Norman French in 1066

base word: a free morpheme to which affixes can be added, usually of Anglo-Saxon origin

closed syllable: a written syllable containing a single vowel letter that ends in one or more consonants. The vowel sound is short.

concept: an idea that links other facts, words, and ideas together into a coherent whole

conjunction: a word that connects a dependent clause to a dependent clause, or a word that connects two independent clauses

consonant: a phoneme (speech sound) that is not a vowel, and that is formed with obstruction of the flow of air with the teeth, lips, or tongue; also called a closed sound in some instructional programs. English has 40 or more consonants.

consonant blend: two or three adjacent consonants before or after the vowel in a syllable, such as st-, spr-, -lk, -mp

consonant digraph: a letter combination that represents one speech sound that is not represented by either letter alone, such as sh, th, wh, ph, ch, ng

consonant-le syllable: a written syllable found at the ends of words such as *paddle*, *single*, and *rubble*

cumulative instruction: teaching that proceeds in additive steps, building on what was previously taught

decodable text: text in which a high proportion of words (around 80 to 90%) comprise sound-symbol relationships that have already been taught; used for the purpose of providing practice with specific decoding skills; a bridge between learning phonics and the application of phonics in independent reading of text

decoding: ability to translate a word from print to speech, usually by employing knowledge of sound-symbol correspondences; also the act of deciphering a new word by sounding it out

dialects: mutually intelligible versions of the same language with systematic differences in phonology, word use, and/or grammatical rules

DIBELS: *Dynamic Indicators of Basic Early Literacy Skills*, by Roland Good and Ruth Kaminski, University of Oregon

dictation: the teacher repeats words, phrases, or sentences slowly while the children practice writing them accurately

digraph: [see consonant digraph]

diphthong: a vowel produced by the tongue shifting position during articulation; a vowel that feels as if it has two parts, especially the vowels spelled <u>ou</u> and <u>oi</u>; some linguistics texts also classify all tense (long) vowels as diphthongs

direct instruction: the teacher defines and teaches a concept, guides children through its application, and arranges for extended guided practice until mastery is achieved

dyslexia: an impairment of reading accuracy and fluency attributable to an underlying phonological processing problem, usually associated with other kinds of language processing difficulties

frequency-controlled text: stories for beginning readers that use very common (high frequency) words over and over, so that the child can learn to read by memorizing a list of "sight" words; phonic patterns in the words are either secondary or irrelevant considerations

high frequency word: a word that occurs very often in written text; a word that is among the 300 to 500 most often used words in English text

generalization: a pattern in the spelling system that generalizes to a substantial family of words

grapheme: a letter or letter combination that spells a phoneme; can be one, two, three, or four letters in English (e, ei, igh, eigh)

idea generator: the thinking process that conjures up ideas as we are writing

inflection: a type of bound morpheme; a grammatical ending that does not change the part of speech of a word but that marks its tense, number, or degree in English (such as *-ed, -s, -ing*)

integrated: when lesson components are interwoven and flow smoothly together

irregular word: one that does not follow common phonic patterns; one that is not a member of a word family, such as *were, was, laugh, been*

long term memory: the memory system that stores information beyond 24 hours

meaning processor: the neural networks that attach meanings to words that have been heard or decoded

morpheme: the smallest meaningful unit of the language

morphology: the study of the meaningful units in the language and how they are combined in word formation

multisyllabic: having more than one syllable

narrative: text that tells about sequences of events, usually with the structure of a story, fiction or nonfiction; often contrasted with expository text that reports factual information and the relationships among ideas

nonsense word: a word that sounds like a real English word and can be sounded out, but that has no assigned meaning, such as *lemvidation*

onset-rime: the natural division of a syllable into two parts, the onset coming before the vowel and the rime including the vowel and what follows it: *pl-an, shr-ill*

orthographic processor: the neural networks responsible for perceiving, storing, and retrieving the letter sequences in words

orthography: a writing system for representing language

phoneme: a speech sound that combines with others in a language system to make words

phoneme awareness (also, phonemic awareness): the conscious awareness that words are made up of segments of our own speech that are represented with letters in an alphabetic orthography

phoneme-grapheme mapping: an activity for showing how letters and letter combinations correspond to the individual speech sounds in a word

phonics: the study of the relationships between letters and the sounds they represent; also used as a descriptor for code-based instruction in reading, e.g., "the phonics approach" or "phonic reading"

phonological awareness: meta-linguistic awareness of all levels of the speech sound system, including word boundaries, stress patterns, syllables, onset-rime units, and phonemes; a more encompassing term than phoneme awareness

phonological processor: a neural network in the frontal and temporal areas of the brain, usually the left cerebral hemisphere, that is specialized for speech sound perception and memory

phonological working memory: the "on-line" memory system that holds speech in mind long enough to extract meaning from it, or that holds onto words during writing; a function of the phonological processor

phonology: the rule system within a language by which phonemes can be sequenced and uttered to make words

pragmatics: the system of rules and conventions for using language and related gestures in a social context

predictable text: a story written for beginning readers that repeats phrase and sentence patterns so that the child has an easier time predicting what the words on the page will say

prefix: a morpheme that precedes a root and that contributes to or modifies the meaning of a word; a common linguistic unit in Latin-based words

reading fluency: speed of reading; the ability to read text with sufficient speed to support comprehension

risk indicator: a task that predicts outcomes on high stakes reading tests

root: a bound morpheme, usually of Latin origin, that cannot stand alone but that is used to form a family of words with related meanings

schwa: the "empty" vowel in an unaccented syllable, such as the last syllables of *circus* and *bagel*

semantics: the study of word and phrase meanings

silent letter spelling: a consonant grapheme with a silent letter and a letter that corresponds to the vocalized sound, such as *kn*, *wr*, *gn*

sound blending: saying the individual phonemes in a word, then putting the sounds together to make a whole word

sound-symbol correspondence: same as phoneme-grapheme correspondence; the rules and patterns by which letters and letter combinations represent speech sounds

speed drills: one-minute timed exercises to build fluency in learned skills

stop: a type of consonant that is spoken with one push of breath and not continued or carried out, including /p/, /b/, /t/, /d/, /k/, /g/

structural analysis: the study of affixes, base words, and roots

suffix: a derivational morpheme added to a root or base that often changes the word's part of speech and that modifies its meaning

syllabic consonants: /m/, /n/, /l/, /r/ can do the job of a vowel and make an unaccented syllable at the ends of words such as *rhythm*, *mitten*, *little*, and *letter*

syllable: the unit of pronunciation that is organized around a vowel; it may or may not have consonants before or after the vowel

text generator: the part of the mind that puts ideas into words as we are writing

transcription: the act of putting words down in writing or typing; the act of producing written words by hand once the mind has generated them

vowel: one of a set of 15 vowel phonemes in English, not including vowel-r combinations; an open phoneme that is the nucleus of every syllable; classified by tongue position and height (high-low, front-back)

whole language: a philosophy of reading instruction that de-emphasizes the importance of phonics and phonology and that emphasizes the importance of learning to recognize words as wholes through encounters in meaningful contexts

writing process approach: instruction in written expression that emphasizes a progression through three major phases, including planning and organizing the piece, writing a draft, getting feedback and revising for publication

word family: a group of words that share a rime [vowel plus the consonants that follow, such as -ame, -ick, -out]

word recognition: the ability to identify the spoken word that a printed word represents, to name the word on the printed page

Appendix A

Answers to Applicable Exercises

Exercise #3: What's Distinctive About Written Language

What is distinctive about language we write? What is distinctive about the communicative relationship between writer and reader? Spend a few minutes listing as many specific linguistic requirements and constraints of formal, conventional written language (academic discourse) as you can.

Level of Language	Written Language	Conversational Speech
Sounds	Represented by print, processed by eye	Processed by ear
Words	No speaker is present for response; no clarification can be requested. Metaphoric and figurative language is more common. More unusual, infrequent words are needed for precise communication.	
Sentences	Sentences must be complete and grammatical. Punctuation and paragraphing are used. Logical connections are signaled in more precise ways.	
Paragraphs	Density of propositions is greater in written language. Redundancy and reference are controlled with word substitutions, pronouns, appositives, and restatements.	
Conventions	Genre conventions govern narrative, expository, and other forms.	

Exercise #6: Writing Skill in Various 1st Graders

Look at the following writing samples from first grade children who have been assessed with the Dynamic Indicators of Basic Early Literacy Skills (DIBELS) and who are in grades K–2. In what way do the words, sentences, and overall quality of language and ideas correspond to the children's status as "low risk," "some risk," and "at risk"?

Case #1, C.P.
1st grader, early January composition. Low risk on DIBELS measures, doing extremely well in letter naming (99th %ile), phoneme segmentation (99th %ile), nonsense word reading (98th %ile) and word use fluency (76th %ile).

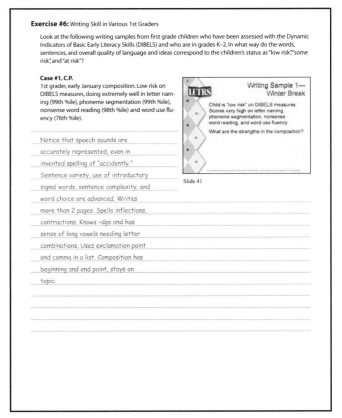
Slide 41

Notice that speech sounds are accurately represented, even in invented spelling of "accidently." Sentence variety, use of introductory signal words, sentence complexity, and word choice are advanced. Writes more than 2 pages. Spells inflections, contractions. Knows –dge and has sense of long vowels needing letter combinations. Uses exclamation point and comma in a list. Composition has beginning and end point, stays on topic.

(continued) **Exercise #6:** Writing Skill in Various 1st Graders

Case #2, N.C.
1st grader, early December composition. At some risk on DIBELS measures: 64th %ile on letter naming, 15th %ile on phoneme segmentation; 21st %ile on nonsense word reading: 44th %ile on word use fluency. Receives ½ hour per day extra small group help with multisensory structured language in addition to classroom Open Court program. Also works on CD Rom with Lindamood LIPS Program and Earobics training in phonology.

Writing Sample #2—
My Thanksgiving
Child "at risk" on DIBELS measures, in "strategic" range.
· Good at naming letters but weak in phoneme segmentation and nonsense word reading.
· Average in word use fluency.
· Is getting small group intervention ½ hr. daily and has improved a lot already.

Slide 42

Is progressing well, but shows mild phonological processing weaknesses; leaves /s/ out of *Thanksgiving,* /n/ out of *lunch;* substitutes voiced /d/ for /t/ in *after;* can't do inventive spelling for *usually.* Writes HOSE for home. Errors are typical for developing 1st graders – FRST for *first* uses /r/ for peak of syllable. No vowel in unaccented final syllable of *favorite.* Also struggles a bit to maintain topic; no ending achieved.

(continued) **Exercise #6:** Writing Skill in Various 1st Graders

Case #3, J.D.
1st grader in January. At risk. Needs intensive support. On an IEP since kindergarten; receives one-one tutoring and small group instruction. Letter naming, 21st %ile; phoneme awareness, 4th %ile; nonsense word reading, 31st %ile; word use fluency, 26th %ile.

Writing Sample #2—
My Thanksgiving
Child "at risk" on DIBELS measures, in "strategic" range
· Good at naming letters but weak in phoneme segmentation and nonsense word reading.
· Average in word use fluency.
· Is getting small group intervention ½ hr. daily and has improved a lot already.

Slide 43

Few words written. Listing of ideas in run-on sentence in perseverative style. Extracts a few salient consonant sounds out of words but does not fully segment them because of underdeveloped phoneme awareness. Leaves the nasal out of *and.* Doesn't elaborate ideas.

I T A M TRUC (I got a remote control truck).

AED A THTHB (and a chalkboard).

AED A MROED (and a motorcycle guy).

AED A SHPS (and slippers).

AED A FPD (and a leapfrog pad).

Wrap-Up Discussion Questions

1. Why are young children vulnerable to overload during writing? What causes overload?

   The attention, memory, language, and executive capacities of a young child are insufficient to juggle all the demands of writing simultaneously. Excessive processing requirements overload the functional writing system.

2. What kinds of tasks, if any, might you want to add to a screening and progress-monitoring assessment of functional writing skills? Are holistic rubrics sufficient for learning what we want to know about developing writers?

   Timed alphabet writing. Timed copying fluency. Speed and accuracy of sound-symbol production. Knowledge of basic spelling vocabulary. Vocabulary level. Ability to generate and tell ideas when writing is not required.

3. What is meant by "balance" in an early writing lesson?

   The distribution of instructional time between structured, systematic practice of component skills and the scaffolded practice of generating and organizing ideas.

4. How can a child who struggles to write be motivated to persist?

   Ensure that letter formation, handwriting fluency, and basic spelling skills are established. Publish or display finished products. Provide sufficient structure for composition success; spend more time equipping the child with a topic, key words, and an organizational plan. Use provocative topics or prompts with emotional substance, rich ideas or imagery. Reward improvement; do not expect perfection. Teach self-talk such as "What I can say, I can write."

Appendix B

Writing Rubrics

Writing Rubrics

Used by permission from the
6 + 1 Traits Model of the
Northwest Regional Educational Laboratory
http://www.nwrel.org/assessment/pdfRubrics/6plus1traits.pdf

Stages of Writing Process	6 + 1 Traits	Underlying Skills
Planning	Ideas	content knowledge, memory, experience, imagination
	Organization	knowledge of genre, logical reasoning ability, goal, focus on the topic
Drafting	Word Choice	size of vocabulary, use of connecting words idioms, figures of speech
	Voice	speaking from conviction, awareness of audience
	Sentence Fluency	sentence variety complex and compound s's "literary" S structure grammatical patterns punctuation, capitalization
Revise/Edit	Conventions	phonological awareness orthographic knowledge (memory for word spellings) handwriting fluency, accuracy
	Presentation	spatial organization communicative intent design

6 + 1 Trait™ Writing
Assessment Scoring Guide

- Ideas
- Organization
- Voice
- Word Choice
- Sentence Fluency
- Conventions
- Presentation

WOW!
exceeds expectations

5   STRONG:
shows control and skill in this trait; many strengths present

4   EFFECTIVE:
on balance, the strengths outweigh the weaknesses; a small amount of revision is needed.

3   DEVELOPING:
strengths and need for revision are about equal; about half-way home

2   EMERGING:
need for revision outweighs strengths; isolated moments hint at what the writer has in mind

1   NOT YET:
a bare beginning; writer not yet showing any control

© Northwest Regional Educational Laboratory, http://www.nwrel.org/assessment/pdfRubrics/6plus1traits.pdf

Ideas and Content
(Development)

5 *This paper is clear and focused. It holds the reader's attention. Relevant anecdotes and details enrich the central theme.*

  A. The topic is **narrow** and **manageable**.

  B. **Relevant**, **telling**, **quality details** give the reader important information that goes **beyond the obvious** or predictable.

  C. Reasonably **accurate details** are present to support the main ideas.

  D. The writer seems to be writing from **knowledge** or **experience**; the ideas are **fresh** and **original**.

  E. The reader's questions are **anticipated and answered**.

  F. **Insight**—an understanding of life and a knack for picking out what is significant—is an indicator of high level performance, though not required.

3 *The writer is beginning to define the topic, even though development is still basic or general.*

  A. The **topic is fairly broad**; however, you can see where the writer is headed.

  B. **Support is attempted**, but doesn't go far enough yet in fleshing out the key issues or story line.

  C. **Ideas are reasonably clear**, though they may not be detailed, personalized, accurate, or expanded enough to show indepth understanding or a strong sense of purpose.

  D. The writer seems to be drawing on knowledge or experience, but **has difficulty going from general observations to specifics**.

  E. The reader is **left with questions**. More information is needed to "fill in the blanks."

  F. The **writer generally stays on the topic** but does not develop a clear theme. The writer has not yet focused the topic past the obvious.

1 *As yet, the paper has no clear sense of purpose or central theme. To extract meaning from the text, the reader must make inferences based on sketchy or missing details. The writing reflects more than one of these problems:*

  A. The writer is **still in search of a topic**, brainstorming, or has not yet decided what the main idea of the piece will be.

  B. Information is **limited** or **unclear** or the **length is not adequate** for development.

  C. The idea is a **simple restatement** of the topic or an **answer** to the question with little or no attention to detail.

  D. The writer has **not begun to define the topic** in a meaningful, personal way.

  E. **Everything seems as important as everything else**; the reader has a hard time sifting out what is important.

  F. The text may be repetitious, or may read like a collection of **disconnected, random thoughts** with no discernable point.

Teaching Beginning Spelling and Writing

Organization

5 *The organization enhances and showcases the central idea or theme. The order, structure, or presentation of information is compelling and moves the reader through the text.*

  A. An **inviting introduction** draws the reader in; a **satisfying conclusion** leaves the reader with a sense of closure and resolution.

  B. **Thoughtful transitions** clearly show how ideas connect.

  C. Details seem to fit where they're placed; **sequencing is logical** and **effective**.

  D. **Pacing is well controlled**; the writer knows when to slow down and elaborate, and when to pick up the pace and move on.

  E. The **title**, if desired, is **original** and captures the central theme of the piece.

  F. Organization **flows so smoothly** the reader hardly thinks about it; the choice of structure matches the **purpose** and **audience**.

3 *The organizational structure is strong enough to move the reader through the text without too much confusion.*

  A. The paper has a **recognizable introduction and conclusion**. The introduction may not create a strong sense of anticipation; the conclusion may not tie-up all loose ends.

  B. **Transitions often work well**; at other times, connections between ideas are fuzzy.

  C. **Sequencing** shows **some logic**, but not under control enough that it consistently supports the ideas. In fact, sometimes it is so predictable and rehearsed that the **structure takes attention away from the content**.

  D. **Pacing is fairly well controlled**, though the writer sometimes lunges ahead too quickly or spends too much time on details that do not matter.

  E. A **title (if desired) is present**, although it may be uninspired or an obvious restatement of the prompt or topic.

  F. The **organization sometimes supports the main point or storyline**; at other times, the reader feels an urge to slip in a transition or move things around.

1 *The writing lacks a clear sense of direction. Ideas, details, or events seem strung together in a loose or random fashion; there is no identifiable internal structure. The writing reflects more than one of these problems:*

  A. There is **no real lead** to set-up what follows, **no real conclusion** to wrap things up.

  B. Connections between ideas are **confusing** or not even present.

  C. **Sequencing needs** lots and lots of **work**.

  D. **Pacing feels awkward**; the writer slows to a crawl when the reader wants to get on with it, and vice versa.

  E. **No title is present** (if requested) or, if present, **does not match** well with the content.

  F. Problems with organization make it **hard for the reader to get a grip** on the main point or storyline.

Voice

5 *The writer speaks directly to the reader in a way that is individual, compelling and engaging. The writer crafts the writing with an awareness and respect for the audience and the purpose for writing.*

  A. The tone of the writing **adds interest** to the message and is **appropriate for the purpose and audience**.

  B. The reader feels a **strong interaction** with the writer, sensing the **person behind the words**.

  C. The writer **takes a risk** by revealing who he or she is consistently throughout the piece.

  D. **Expository or persuasive** writing reflects a **strong commitment** to the topic by showing **why** the **reader needs to know this** and why he or she should care.

  E. **Narrative** writing is **honest**, **personal**, and **engaging** and makes you **think about**, and **react to**, the author's ideas and point of view.

3 *The writer seems sincere but not fully engaged or involved. The result is pleasant or even personable, but not compelling.*

  A. The writer seems aware of an audience but discards personal insights in favor of **obvious generalities**.

  B. The writing communicates in an **earnest, pleasing, yet safe** manner.

  C. Only **one or two moments here or there** intrigue, delight, or move the reader. These places may **emerge strongly for a line or two, but quickly fade away**.

  D. **Expository or persuasive** writing **lacks consistent engagement** with the topic to build credibility.

  E. **Narrative** writing is **reasonably sincere**, but doesn't reflect unique or individual perspective on the topic.

1 *The writer seems indifferent, uninvolved, or distanced from the topic and/or the audience. As a result, the paper reflects more than one of the following problems:*

  A. The writer is **not concerned with the audience**. The writer's style is a **complete mismatch** for the intended reader or the writing is **so short** that little is accomplished beyond introducing the topic.

  B. The writer speaks in a kind of **monotone** that flattens all potential highs or lows of the message.

  C. The writing is **humdrum and "risk-free."**

  D. The writing is **lifeless or mechanical**; depending on the topic, it may be overly technical or jargonistic.

  E. The development of the topic is **so limited** that **no point of view is present**—zip, zero, zilch, nada.

Word Choice

5 *Words convey the intended message in a precise, interesting, and natural way. The words are powerful and engaging.*

    A. Words are **specific** and **accurate**. It is easy to understand just what the writer means.

    B. **Striking words and phrases** often catch the reader's eye and linger in the reader's mind.

    C. Language and phrasing is **natural**, **effective**, and **appropriate** for the audience.

    D. **Lively verbs** add energy while **specific nouns** and **modifiers** add depth.

    E. Choices in language **enhance** the **meaning** and **clarify** understanding.

    F. **Precision** is obvious. The writer has taken care to put just the right word or phrase in just the right spot.

3 *The language is functional, even if it lacks much energy. It is easy to figure out the writer's meaning on a general level.*

    A. Words are **adequate and correct in a general sense**, and they support the meaning by not getting in the way.

    B. Familiar **words and phrases communicate** but rarely capture the reader's imagination.

    C. **Attempts at colorful language** show a willingness to stretch and grow but sometimes reach beyond the audience (thesaurus overload!).

    D. Despite a **few successes**, the writing is marked by **passive verbs**, **everyday nouns**, and **mundane modifiers**.

    E. The word and phrases are **functional** with only **one or two fine moments**.

    F. The words may be **refined in a couple of places**, but the language looks more like **the first thing that popped into the writer's mind**.

1 *The writer demonstrates a limited vocabulary or has not searched for words to convey specific meaning.*

    A. Words are so **nonspecific and distracting** that only a **very limited meaning** comes through.

    B. Problems with language **leave** the **reader wondering**. Many of the **words** just **don't work** in this piece.

    C. Audience has not been considered. **Language is used incorrectly** making the message secondary to the misfires with the words.

    D. **Limited vocabulary** and/or **misused parts of speech** seriously impair understanding.

    E. Words and phrases are so **unimaginative** and **lifeless** that they detract from the meaning.

    F. **Jargon or clichés** distract or mislead. **Redundancy** may distract the reader.

© Northwest Regional Educational Laboratory, http://www.nwrel.org/assessment/pdfRubrics/6plus1traits.pdf

Sentence Fluency

5 *The writing has an easy flow, rhythm, and cadence. Sentences are well built, with strong and varied structure that invites expressive oral reading.*

   A. Sentences are constructed in a way that underscores and enhances the **meaning**.

   B. Sentences **vary in length as well as structure**. Fragments, if used, add style. Dialogue, if present, sounds natural.

   C. **Purposeful** and **varied sentence beginnings** add variety and energy.

   D. The use of **creative and appropriate connectives** between sentences and thoughts shows how each relates to, and builds upon, the one before it.

   E. The writing has **cadence**; the writer has thought about the sound of the words as well as the meaning. The first time you read it aloud is a breeze.

3 *The text hums along with a steady beat, but tends to be more pleasant or businesslike than musical, more mechanical than fluid.*

   A. Although sentences may not seem artfully crafted or musical, **they get the job done in a routine fashion**.

   B. Sentences are **usually constructed correctly**; they **hang together**; they are **sound**.

   C. **Sentence beginnings** are not ALL alike; **some variety is attempted**.

   D. The reader sometimes has to **hunt for clues** (e.g., connecting words and phrases like *however, therefore, naturally, after a while, on the other hand, to be specific, for example, next, first of all, but as it turned out, although,* etc.) that show how sentences interrelate.

   E. **Parts** of the text **invite expressive oral reading**; others may be stiff, awkward, choppy, or gangly.

1 *The reader has to practice quite a bit in order to give this paper a fair interpretive reading. The writing reflects more than one of the following problems:*

   A. Sentences are **choppy, incomplete, rambling or awkward**; they need work. **Phrasing does not sound natural.** The patterns may create a sing-song rhythm, or a chop-chop cadence that lulls the reader to sleep.

   B. There is little to **no "sentence sense"** present. Even if this piece was flawlessly edited, the sentences would not hang together.

   C. Many **sentences begin the same way**—and may follow the same patterns (e.g., *subject-verb-object*) in a monotonous pattern.

   D. **Endless connectives** (*and, and so, but then, because,* and *then,* etc.) or a **complete lack of connectives** create a massive jumble of language.

   E. The text **does not invite expressive oral reading**.

Conventions

5 *The writer demonstrates a good grasp of standard writing conventions (e.g., spelling, punctuation, capitalization, grammar, usage, paragraphing) and uses conventions effectively to enhance readability. Errors tend to be so few that just minor touch-ups would get this piece ready to publish.*

A. **Spelling is generally correct**, even on more difficult words.

B. The **punctuation is accurate**, even creative, and guides the reader through the text.

C. A thorough understanding and consistent application of **capitalization** skills are present.

D. **Grammar and usage are correct** and contribute to clarity and style.

E. **Paragraphing tends to be sound** and reinforces the organizational structure.

F. The writer may **manipulate conventions** for stylistic effect—and it works! The piece is very close to being ready to publish.

> **GRADES 7 AND UP ONLY:** *The writing is sufficiently complex to allow the writer to show skill in using a wide range of conventions. For writers at younger ages, the writing shows control over those conventions that are grade/age appropriate.*

3 *The writer shows reasonable control over a limited range of standard writing conventions. Conventions are sometimes handled well and enhance readability; at other times, errors are distracting and impair readability.*

A. **Spelling** is usually **correct or reasonably phonetic on common words**, but more difficult words are problematic.

B. **End punctuation is usually correct**; internal punctuation (*commas, apostrophes, semicolons, dashes, colons, parentheses*) is sometimes missing/wrong.

C. **Most words are capitalized correctly**; control over more sophisticated capitalization skills may be spotty.

D. **Problems with grammar or usage are not serious** enough to distort meaning but may not be correct or accurately applied all of the time.

E. **Paragraphing is attempted** but may run together or begin in the wrong places.

F. **Moderate editing** (a little of this, a little of that) would be required to polish the text for publication.

1 *Errors in spelling, punctuation, capitalization, usage, and grammar and/or paragraphing repeatedly distract the reader and make the text difficult to read. The writing reflects more than one of these problems:*

A. **Spelling errors are frequent**, even on common words.

B. **Punctuation** (including terminal punctuation) is often **missing or incorrect**.

C. **Capitalization** is **random** and only the easiest rules show awareness of correct use.

D. **Errors in grammar or usage are very noticeable**, frequent, and affect meaning.

E. **Paragraphing is missing, irregular, or so frequent** (every sentence) that it has no relationship to the organizational structure of the text.

F. The reader must **read once to decode**, then again for meaning. **Extensive editing** (virtually every line) would be required to polish the text for publication.

Presentation

(Optional)

5 *The form and presentation of the text enhances the ability for the reader to understand and connect with the message. It is pleasing to the eye.*

  A. If handwritten (either cursive or printed), the **slant is consistent**, letters are clearly formed, **spacing is uniform** between words, and the text is easy to read.

  B. If word-processed, there is **appropriate use of fonts and font sizes** which invites the reader into the text.

  C. The use of **white space** on the page (spacing, margins, etc.) allows the intended audience to easily focus on the text and message without distractions. There is just the right amount of balance of white space and text on the page. The formatting suits the purpose for writing.

  D. The use of a **title, side heads, page numbering, bullets,** and evidence of correct use of a style sheet (when appropriate) makes it easy for the reader to access the desired information and text. These markers allow the hierarchy of information to be clear to the reader.

  E. When appropriate to the purpose and audience, there is **effective integration of text and illustrations, charts, graphs, maps, tables, etc.** There is clear alignment between the text and visuals. The visuals support and clarify important information or key points made in the text.

3 *The writer's message is understandable in this format.*

  A. **Handwriting is readable**, although there may be **discrepancies in letter shape and form, slant, and spacing** that may make some words or passages easier to read than others.

  B. **Experimentation with fonts and font sizes** is successful in some places, but begins to get fussy and cluttered in others. The **effect is not consistent** throughout the text.

  C. While margins may be present, **some text may crowd the edges**. Consistent spacing is applied, although a different choice may make text more accessible (e.g., single, double, or triple spacing).

  D. Although some markers are present (titles, numbering, bullets, side heads, etc.), they are not used to their fullest potential as a guide for the reader to access the greatest meaning from the text.

  E. An **attempt is made to integrate visuals** and the text although the connections may be limited.

1 *The reader receives a garbled message due to problems relating to the presentation of the text.*

  A. Because the letters are irregularly slanted, formed inconsistently, or incorrectly, and the spacing is unbalanced or not even present, it is **very difficult to read and understand the text**.

  B. The writer has gone **wild with multiple fonts and font sizes**. It is a major distraction to the reader.

  C. The **spacing is random and confusing** to the reader. There may be little or no white space on the page.

  D. **Lack of markers** (title, page, numbering, bullets, side heads, etc.) leaves the reader wondering how one section connects to another and why the text is organized in this manner on the page.

  E. The visuals do not support or further illustrate key ideas presented in the text. They may be **misleading, indecipherable, or too complex** to be understood.

Language Essentials
for Teachers of
Reading and
Spelling

Appendix C

Additional Writing Samples

From Mid-February, Mrs. Bird's First Grade
Emily Dickinson Elementary
Lake Washington School District

Program in Use: *Write Well* by Marilyn Sprick
Sopris West Educational Services

Name _____   Date 2-13-02

My Favorite Animal.

My horsey ivs me rides.

My horse cun run.

My horse cun eatrand
drenck. I love my hors.
drink   horse.

Name _____   Date 5-13-02

My Favorite animal
hers   a   dog. Oe   liecks
   is ?   H   likes

to play   al_t.   He liecks
              a lot :   likes

to eat   snow.Oae   liecks
                       He   likes

play   catch.I   lieck   dogs
                          like

be_as   thae   play   al_t.
because   they   a lot :

Name _____ Date 2-13-02

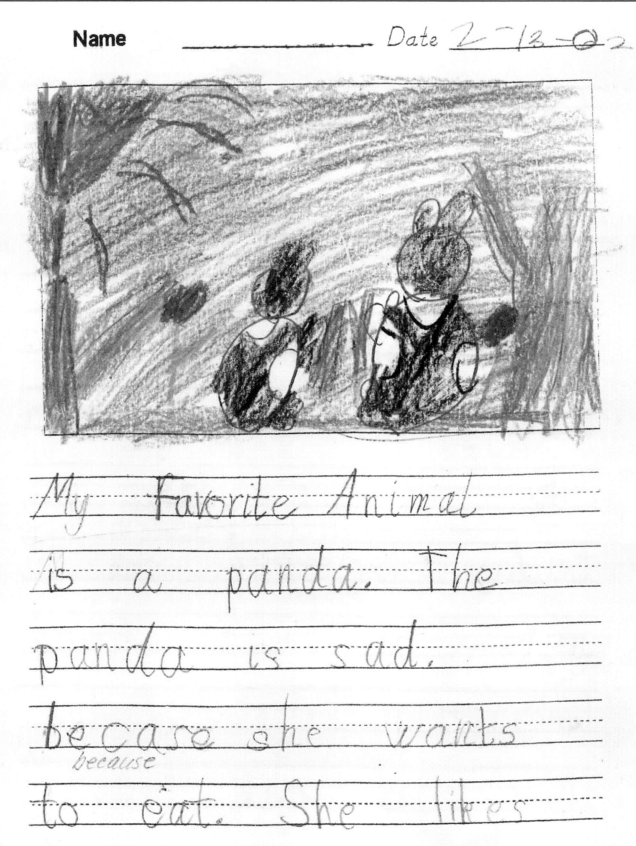

My Favorite Animal
is a panda. The
panda is sad.
becase she wants
because
to eat. She likes

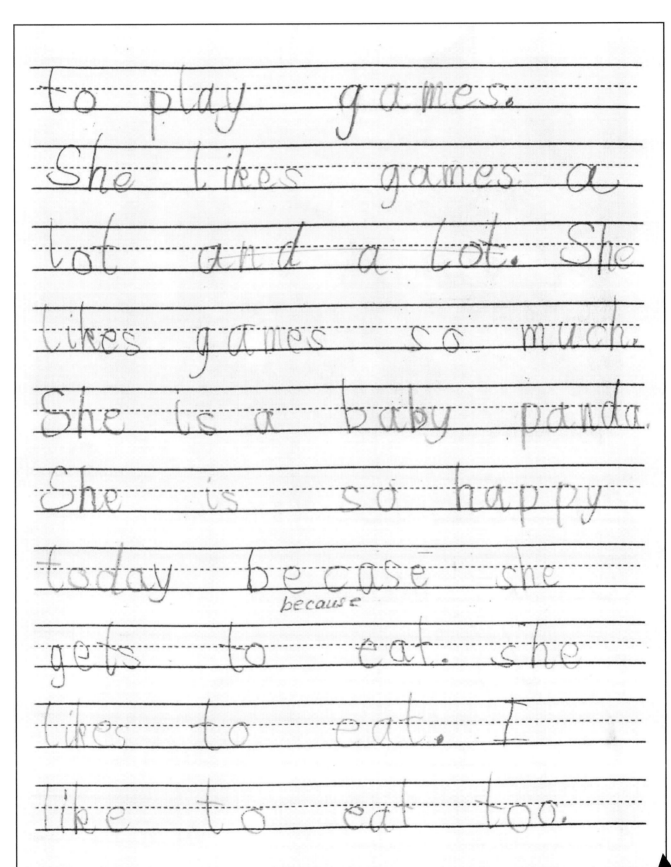

to play games.
She likes games a
lot and a lot. She
likes games so much.
She is a baby panda.
She is so happy
today becase she
                  because
gets to eat. she
likes to eat. I
like to eat too.

Name _____ Date 2 — 13 — 02

My Favorite Animal

One day a baby panda

woke up. She was all pink.

her name was Amanda.

Then Amanda disided to

decided

go play. But when Amanda

got to the playpen she

notesd that she cuodint

notised   *couldn't*

reach the bamboo. But

even wers! She almost

worse , s

got stept on by a bigger

stepped

panda! Little Amanda

ran as fast as her little

legs cuod take her and

legs   *could*

ran all the way home

wer mom had bamboo waiting

where

for her.   Wonderful story, Amanda!

Appendix D

Goals for Learning Writing Skills, Grades K-2

Goals for Learning Writing Skills, Grades K-2

Ideas and Their Organization

Kindergarten Goals (Oral Language)

1. Given a series of pictures, orally retell a story or sequence of events in order.
2. Orally give a sequence of directions for a common activity.

First Grade Goals

1. Write several sentences in a logical sequence or narrative sequence.
2. Use signal words to indicate the order of events or ideas.
3. Write complete sentences with descriptive elaboration of the subject and predicate.
4. Categorize ideas and use simple semantic webs or graphics to show how ideas are related.

Second Grade Goals

1. Write several expository paragraphs about a topic that follow the structure of topic sentence, details, and concluding sentence.
2. Write a personal narrative and a fictional narrative; plan with a simple story frame.
3. Write a friendly letter and a persuasive letter.

Vocabulary: Word Choice and Word Use

Kindergarten Goals (Oral Language)

1. Use prepositions showing spatial relationships (under, over).
2. Name body parts.
3. Name colors.
4. Name common objects and parts of objects.
5. Name the months and the days of the week.
6. Follow instructional language of the classroom.
7. Identify opposites.

First Grade Goals (Oral and Written Language)

1. Identify opposites in word pairs.
2. Categorize words and ideas and explain how the words are related.
3. Substitute stronger words for overused, bland, nonspecific nouns and verbs.

Second Grade Goals (Written Language)

1. Place coordinating conjunctions between parts of a compound sentence.

2. Use subordinating conjunctions to introduce clauses in a complex sentence.

3. Choose specific nouns and strong verbs to elaborate ideas.

Sentences: Grammar and Conventional Usage

Kindergarten Goals (Oral Language)

1. Use the correct form of irregular verbs such as go (went), have (had, has), do (did), think (thought), take (took).

2. Use the correct article with a noun (a, an, the).

3. Speak in complete sentences.

4. Use verbs that agree with nouns (he doesn't).

5. Use comparative and superlative forms with common adverbs and adjectives.

6. Use personal pronouns in compounds (Dad and I went to the park; he and I enjoyed it. The ball belongs to him and me.).

First Grade Goals

1. Write in complete sentences; join compounds with "and" and "but."

2. Write the correct form of irregular verbs.

3. Write sentences with correct subject-verb agreement (when no words intervene).

4. Write comparative (–er) and superlative (–est) endings with common vocabulary.

5. Maintain consistent verb tense in compositions.

6. Use correct pronouns with clear referents.

7. Use complete prepositional phrases.

8. Use the appropriate article (the, a, an) before nouns.

9. Write complete answers for questions. Formulate questions from statements.

10. Identify four basic sentence types.

Second Grade Goals

1. Write the correct form of less common irregular verbs.

2. Use correct subject-verb agreement, even when other words intervene.

3. Use comparative and superlative forms, including "more" and "most."

4. Avoid using double negatives.

5. Use conventional personal pronouns in subject and object positions.

6. Use consistent verb tense throughout paragraphs.

7. Vary sentence type in a composition.

Sentences: Punctuation

Kindergarten Goals

1. Use a period at the end of a statement.

2. Use an apostrophe in a common contraction (I'm, don't).

First Grade Goals

1. Use a question mark at the end of a question beginning with who, what, when, where, why, or how.

2. Use an exclamation point for an exclamation.

3. Use periods at the ends of statements and in abbreviations such as Mr., Ms., and Dr.

4. Place an apostrophe in a contraction and explain what it stands for.

5. Use a comma to separate city and state in own address.

6. Use a comma to separate day from month in dates.

Second Grade Goals

1. Use a period at the end of a statement, a question mark at the end of a question, and an exclamation point at the end of an exclamation or an imperative.

2. Use an apostrophe to show possession or to mark a contraction.

3. Use a comma to separate items in a list, the parts of a compound sentence, and to separate city and state in any address.

4. Use periods with abbreviations for Street, Road, Lane, Place, Avenue.

Sentences: Capitalization

Kindergarten Goals

1. Capitalize "I" and the first letter of one's name.
2. Differentiate between upper and lower case letters.

First Grade Goals

1. Capitalize "I" and the first letter of a sentence.
2. Capitalize the names of people, names of the days and months, and the names of places in family addresses.
3. Capitalize the names of holidays.
4. Capitalize titles of books and compositions.

Second Grade Goals

1. Capitalize first and last names.
2. Capitalize city and state in own address.
3. Capitalize formal names of family members (Aunt Betty).
4. Capitalize holidays.
5. Capitalize common street names.
6. Identify when words should not be capitalized.
7. Capitalize titles of familiar books.

Alphabetics and Handwriting

Kindergarten Goals

1. Recite the alphabet in order.
2. Name upper and lower case letters.
3. Match upper and lower case letters.
4. Copy the alphabet sequence with 3-D letters.
5. Copy the alphabet, upper and lower case, on lined paper.
6. Write any letter to dictation.
7. Copy simple sentences accurately.

First Grade Goals

1. Use legible manuscript letter formation spaced within given lines on primary writing paper.
2. Write the whole lower case alphabet with satisfactory fluency (in less than one minute).
3. Write the whole upper case alphabet with satisfactory fluency.
4. Copy sentences on a paper with satisfactory fluency.

Second Grade Goals

1. Alphabetize to the second letter in a list of words.

2. Write the manuscript alphabet legibly and with fluency.

3. Begin the transition to cursive handwriting.

Spelling

Kindergarten Goals

1. Segment simple words with two and three phonemes.

2. Write a conventional grapheme for each speech sound in English.

3. Write regular, closed syllables with two and three phonemes, using high probability sound-letter correspondences.

4. Write unknown words with typical inventive spellings showing awareness of most speech sounds ("illustrated by"—ilashtradid bi)

5. Write common irregular words from the 50 most often used words in English.

6. Use spelling knowledge in writing short compositions.

First Grade Goals

1. Spell common closed syllables with three and four phonemes, including digraphs, blends, and "position" spellings (–ck, –ll, –ss, –ff); simple Vce syllables; words with long vowels ee, ea, ai, and oa; words with /i/ spelled y; and common words with endings –ing, –s, and –ed.

2. Spell the first 100 most common words in written English in dictated lists or sentences.

3. Write the correct choice among common homophones—to, too, two, etc.

4. Write contractions with an apostrophe, and common abbreviations with a period.

5. Give a readable and accurate phonetic spelling for words that have not been taught.

6. Use spelling knowledge to edit and proofread work by self and others.

Second Grade Goals

1. Spell in dictations the most common 200 words in English.

2. Apply knowledge of consonant spelling patterns including hard and soft c and g; –ge and –dge; –ch and –tch; and qu.

3. Spell regular long vowel syllables including vowel teams, Vce, and open syllables in two-syllable words.

4. Spell vowel-r combinations ir, ur, er, or, ar.

5. Spell diphthongs by pattern and position, including –ou/ow, and –oi/oy.

6. Spell past tense (three sounds for –ed) and plural endings (–s and –es) on common vocabulary.

7. With prompting, apply the consonant doubling, change y to i, and drop silent e spelling rules for adding suffixes.

8. Spell most common contractions.

9. Use appropriate homophones for common vocabulary.

10. Apply spelling knowledge in proofreading and editing.

NOTES

NOTES

NOTES

NOTES

NOTES

NOTES